'Frances Cornford excels at the short epigrammatic poem, but also probes deeply into human emotions, portraying with truthful sympathy a variety of characters, from the scholar, breathing his rarefied air, to the peasant woman who sits sewing through the tragic events of her life.'
ANNE RIDLER

'Frances Cornford's poems surprise and illuminate. They capture the immediate moment with strong sensuous detail, but also convey a feeling of passing time and loss: the "calm-struck soldier leaning on the bridge" will vanish, leaving everything as it always was. Her poems are compelling in their directness, clarity and in the breadth of their resolution. One senses the searching, generous spirit of the poet in the work. It speaks to us today.'
JANE DURAN

FRANCES CORNFORD

Selected Poems

Edited by
JANE DOWSON

with a memoir by
HUGH CORNFORD

and illustrations by
Gwen Raverat and Christopher Cornford

London
ENITHARMON PRESS
1996

First published in 1996
by the Enitharmon Press
36 St George's Avenue
London N7 0HD

Distributed in Europe
by Password (Books) Ltd.
23 New Mount Street
Manchester, M4 4DE

Distributed in the USA and Canada
by Dufour Editions Inc.
PO Box 7, Chester Springs
PA 19425-0007, USA

ISBN 1 870612 87 6

Typeset in 10pt Bembo by Bryan Williamson, Frome,
and printed by The Cromwell Press, Wiltshire

Poetry Books by Frances Cornford

Illustrations in the Text

The woodcuts reproduced on pages vi, xi, xxv, xxxvii, xxxviii, 12, 13, 16, 60 and 64 are by Gwen Raverat, from *Mountains and Molehills* (1934).

The drawings reproduced on pages 9, 31, 35, 37 and 62 are by Christopher Cornford, from *Travelling Home and Other Poems* (1948).

Acknowledgements

Hugh Cornford, in consultation with members and friends of the family, has been instrumental in the selection of the poems. He has also been an endless source of information: I am grateful for his co-operation from beginning to end in providing and checking details and in completing his memoir. Timothy Rogers and Anne Harvey have given invaluable encouragement and support. I would also like to thank Frances Spalding and Jane Duran for their interest in the project and shared appreciation of the poems.

Permission to print the poems has been granted by Hugh Cornford. Permission to reproduce the woodcuts by Gwen Raverat has kindly been given by Sophie Gurney and Elizabeth Hambro and for the *Poems from the Russian* by the Salaman family.

J.D.

Contents

The poems marked with an asterisk were not included by Frances Cornford in her *Collected Poems* (1954)

Introduction
Jane Dowson

I came across Frances Cornford when investigating women's poetry between the wars; in the course of this research, I discovered twenty or so women who were successful poets, but who have been neglected in literary history. Many of these poets, like Sylvia Townsend Warner and Anna Wickham, have recently been rediscovered and their poems have been collected and reprinted. Frances Cornford's poems, however, have been out of print for thirty years even though she was well known as a poet from the 1920s onwards, up until the time when she received the Queen's Gold Medal for Poetry in 1959 and her posthumous collection *On a Calm Shore* (1960).[1] Her nine books of poetry were reviewed seriously on publication and sold well. Throughout her life she published poems in periodicals and anthologies; she won prizes and judged poetry competitions; she gave readings and lectures on poetry, and her *Collected Poems* (1954) was the third Choice of the Poetry Book Society. There is still a continuing appreciation of her poetry and on the rare occasions that her books arrive in second-hand bookshops they quickly disappear, especially in her home city of Cambridge.

Frances Cornford was evidently respected as a poet in her lifetime. In *Some Contemporary Poets* (1920), Harold Monro, who with his wife Alida ran The Poetry Bookshop in Devonshire Street, London – a centre for discussing and marketing poetry – includes her in his conspectus of current British poetry as someone who wrote a lot and 'then appears to have stopped'.[2] This was not actually the case, and is contradicted by a reviewer of Thomas Moult's *Best Poems of 1924* who cited Frances Cornford in 'a list of names which attract attention even before their contributions are savoured'.[3] She published throughout the 1920s and *Different Days* (1928) was the first of the Hogarth Living Poets series published by Virginia and Leonard Woolf. In 1933, the Editor of *The Listener* referred to her as 'a household name' when including her in a list of prizewinners.[4] She won prizes in competitions run by the BBC and *The New Statesman and Nation*, including several awards from the latter for the best translation of a poem.[5] She usually signed herself by her initials 'F.C.C.'

One of the reasons for the decline of her reputation since her death in 1960 has been that the poems have been mistaken as naïve. The assumed simplicity of the poems' speakers are, however, a device by which she can 'turn things over', as the writer Naomi Mitchison put it.[6] In another of the several letters of appreciation which she received on the publication of *Collected Poems* (1954), her talent was identified as the 'powers of expression and of drawing pictures in a few words...the true power of sympathetic insight [which] can look under the surface of things'.[7] On reading her manuscripts in the British Library and Bodleian Library I discovered more examples of how Frances Cornford's poetry has drawn attention and has had a wide appeal; the periodicals in which her poems were published include *The New York Saturday Review*, as well as many British magazines and journals, from *The Spectator* to *Country Life* or *Time and Tide*. Various poems, such as 'Casualties', 'Soldiers on the Platform', and 'Parting in Wartime' were set to music[8] and 'The Watch' is listed in a New York concert programme.[9] There are permission requests to include her poems in anthologies of verse as far afield as Hungary and India and 'Grand Ballet' was used for an Eistedfodd reading test.

Looking through her papers, I also became fascinated by the poet herself. Frances Cornford's letters, journals and notebooks demonstrate that she was a prolific correspondent, that she was acquainted with many well-known artists and writers, that she was devoted to her family and friends, and that she suffered from depression and a sense of failure as a mother, during the 1930s in particular, and that she took reading and writing poetry very seriously – there is a record of her going to meet with Thomas Hardy in 1910.[10] From the papers I gained the impression of a striking personality with a sense of humour and of a woman who could write with sensitivity to her audience, but in whom there was also a recurring undercurrent of unhappiness. This is particularly evident from her journals, from the entry as a sixteen-year-old, 'I am ugly, selfish and utterly despicable' to 'I'm frightened because you say I'm not neurotic... But I seem to myself to be only keeping my head just above water and complete neuroticism – a period comes and I dip under again', when she was forty-eight.[11] This latter entry was written during the middle of her three long depressions and corresponds to the poem 'She Warns Him':

> I am a book, a book with a cover,
> And nothing at all inside.

This poem illustrates the way in which the *appearance* of simplicity is what the poetry is about; an astute critic identified a 'macabre' aspect to the poems,[12] whereas readers who are only familiar with the anthologised poems – which are usually her early ones – take the simplicity at face value and miss the undertow.

In spite of, and during, the bouts of depression, Frances Cornford's correspondence indicates that she wished to enrich the lives of others; the letters which she received usually contain some thanks for her sympathy and kindness, thoughtful words or a gift. In her letters, she usually projects herself into the situation of the recipient and says little about her own circumstances. She clearly valued her relationships and yet suffered from the tension experienced by many woman writers who tried to give themselves to their families and friendships, to hospitality, and also to their work. In the manuscript of a talk entitled 'Views and Recollections of a Sunday Poet', she wrote that although all poets needed an additional profession to writing, 'none requires the expense of spirit as domestic life does on a woman'.[13] It would seem that for Frances Cornford, the tension was at times acute; one clue to this is in her notebooks and literary papers, where she often refers to her wish to be taken seriously as a poet. To this end, she drafted her work endlessly and sought the advice of critics amongst her friends, family and literary acquaintances.

The degree of self-confidence about her ability as a poet seemed to fluctuate. From the beginning she was discouraged by her sons, John and Christopher, who appear to have been more generous in their criticisms than in their praise.[14] She, however, encouraged John with his poetry, and refused an offer to publish poems with Faber in favour of a project to combine her poems with Christopher's illustrations; this was achieved in *Travelling Home* (1948) and *On a Calm Shore* (1960), both published by the Cresset Press. Typically, and quite rightly, she was keen to point out that the illustrations were not just companions to the poems but, albeit inspired by the poems, works of art in their own right.[15]

In choosing the poems I have collaborated with her son Hugh, who has tried to represent the poet's wishes; we have wanted to indicate both her range and characteristics, and also to redress the myth that she is the purveyor of 'precious' verses. I have maintained a chronological order, although I would want to question the extent to which development in her work is palpable. She herself denounced her early 'poeticism' and blamed her upbringing for inculcating the discipline of metrical evenness, 'Kiplingesque and clichéd'; she believed that she had grown up in a poor state of poetical 'ambience' with 'finger thumping poets as Sassoon called them'.[16] She disliked her early work because of the 'Georgian idiom', with its 'faded poeticisms and jog trot rhythms', by which she was surrounded and 'unconsciously used'. She charted her development through the Cambridge poems, from 'Autumn Morning at Cambridge' – 'marred by the turgid metres' – to 'Travelling Home', 'In the Backs' and 'Gone Down', which has the 'more casual tone of voice' for which she strove; at the same time she believed that they all reflected a 'sense of the impermanence of all human relationships' which ran through her work.[17] Although she worked at resisting the 'rhythms which were well sunk into [my] generation's unconscious',[18] she still believed that rhyme and rhythm were important. She disliked affectation – 'I cannot *bear* in poetry all those abstracts – the ineffable and eternal etc. which for me it is largely the business of poetry to suggest to the imagination in concrete images' and valued the sincerity apparent in the authenticity of the younger generation, whereas the Edwardians had substituted 'polish' for authenticity.[19]

Any attempt to make categories by theme or to structure the poems into chronological stages of poetic development will inevitably only work to a limited extent: the poems in *On a Calm Shore*, for example, at times register a maturity and unprecedented freedom in versification, but some are similar to earlier poems. As suggested by the headings in *On a Calm Shore* – 'Time', 'Children', 'Night and Day', 'Love', 'Places and Seasons', 'Transience' – there *is* a sense of the cycle of life and the seasons, and a strong sense of place in the poems, but these usually foreground the human interest where the complex mind of the observed or observer is the subject of the poem. 'A Glimpse', for example, is about her husband, and put with 'The Scholar' it reads of both unity and separateness and it is clear that the speaker's attitude to academia is not unequivocal. 'In the Backs', at first glance, can appear to celebrate the 'sacred air' where Milton, Chaucer, Herbert, Herrick, and Gray once trod, but in the end it is about loss and mortality: 'too many of the dead, some I knew well'. This sensitivity to separation and death fuels the anti-heroic treatment of public achievement, whether academic or military. 'Parting in Wartime' is, for example, a sleight-of-hand deflation of mythologised classical heroes who are equated with the couple and their baby in the Euston Station waiting-room.

Nijinsky is mentioned in three poems and is a significant symbol of mental breakdown; in Nijinsky's case, it was a response to war – the 'chaos of the night' mentioned in 'Autumn Blitz'. The poem 'Grand Ballet' recounts an occasion when Frances and her husband saw the famous ballet dancer – an occasion upon which she often dwelt, wondering what would happen to such a memory when she died. The Nijinsky image represents the fine line between sanity and insanity or life and death which features in several poems – see for example 'Bedroom Dawn'. The fragility of joy – the 'whirl of love and hate' – also punctures several of the love poems in *On a Calm Shore* and the cycles of nature are not necessarily perceived as reasons to hope; in 'Childhood', for example, there is a humorous, but unsettling, fusion of childhood and age:

> ... she was helplessly old,
> As I was helplessly young.

This poem was actually based on an encounter with an elderly visitor at Aunt Etty's (Henrietta's) house.[20] Other subjects often derive from particular people: 'The Corner of the Field' is about her son Hugh and 'The Grandson Dresses Up' names John's son James as the child.

Reading through the poems it is striking how many refer to death; this sense that 'in the midst of life we are in death' ('Soldiers on the Platform') occurs throughout the poems, from the very early 'The Watch' to 'Exeunt Omnes' which finishes *On a Calm Shore*. The former is disconcerting when it is a child who is almost consumed by a death-wish – 'death, come quick'. Even the light-hearted jibe at the murderous acts of critics is in epitaph form ('Epitaph for a Reviewer'). By contextualising the poetry in terms of the poet's experiences, it is not surprising that death was a preoccupation: belonging to a large family – her father was one of six children – Frances Cornford inevitably encountered deaths as a regular occurrence, as suggested by the poem on the death of Aunt Sarah ('At the End') and 'A Recollection', which is based upon an actual childhood event of being told of the death of a family friend; more pertinent was Frances' mother's death when she was seventeen. In the First World War she lost her friend Rupert Brooke, amongst others – the poem 'Contemporaries', dated April 1915, was originally titled 'No Immortality'; her father died in 1925, her son John was killed in the Spanish Civil War (1936), and other friends and relatives in the Second World War. Her husband died in 1943 – he is most explicitly commemorated in 'The Scholar'. In the light of these losses, poems like 'Missing', and 'An Old Friend', originally titled 'The Dead One', read as acutely personal, as well as expressions of the universal experiences of grief.

Her journals indicate that from an early age Frances Cornford was dogged by questions of the origins and purpose of life. A journal entry dated 1901 asks, 'How can people unsymbolically still believe in Adam and Eve after my grandfather?'; in 1915 she wrote to Gilbert

Murray that she would rather be 'a most degraded form of Christian than a Stoic', after hearing a lecture on the Stoics by her husband. In the 1930s she was reading Carl Jung, and in the 1940s she was still discussing the relative virtues of the Stoics and Christians, although she had by that time become reconciled to the Christian creed.[21] Responses to her poetry, from the first volume *Poems* (1910) onwards, identified her ability to articulate common but unspoken thoughts and to represent emotions unemotionally.[22] Roger E. Fry, a pupil of her father, wrote to say that her poems 'unlocked a lot of things that had always been imprisoned' and 'G' wrote, 'You have a way of tightening the heart strings – they are v. good too in the coldest technical sense'.[23] The best poems both articulate what is often unspoken and have a quality of evocation. The critic and writer David Garnett perceived that this combination of telling and suggesting developed during her career; on the publication of *Collected Poems* he commended her later work in particular because it was more evocative, pointing to 'something greater', whereas the earlier poems could be 'held in the hand'.[24] This perception of development in her poetry is a common one, although the reproduction of mixed feelings which unsettle the reader is evident throughout. At the rawest level, these mixed feelings are the combination of cheerfulness and melancholy or of acceptance and resistance to the condition of being human. This combination of moods is well illustrated in 'Ode on the Whole Duty of Parents' or 'The Sick Queen'. The underlying melancholy of 'Ode' is the recognition that 'all the things a fairy story tells' are powerful ideals which are presented to children but which are not achievable; similarly, 'The Sick Queen', which was written about the time of the middle depression (1934–40), draws upon fairy tale to depict the fact that the idealised figures of fairy stories are flawed and vulnerable characters in real life; this queen represents the mother who cannot live up to her own or her children's expectations and as a result is undergoing 'The long failing fight,/On and on with pain.'

Fairy tales were important to Frances Cornford, perhaps because they embody the distinction between hope and quotidian reality, especially as experienced by the developing child. The 'Fairy-Tale Idyll for Two Voices' is a lyrical narrative which seems to yearn for mythical fairytale fulfilment or prelapsarian perfection:

> O sing and tell of this, and tell no more
> But how, as on the first created day
> All things were new

Again, albeit under a cloak of amusement, nostalgia for the 'fairy story place' is contrasted to the social world of convention and non-communication in 'Journeys End in Lovers' Meeting':

> I used to wish when I was 17
>
> . . .
>
> That I could find that fairy-story place
> Where there is everything that might have been

In this poem, Hell is conceived of as the place of missed opportunities. A missed opportunity is at the centre of several poems, whether it is the chance to have said sorry to someone now dead ('The Benefactors'; 'The Quarrel') or the chance of a different way of life, the road not taken, as in 'The Princess and the Gypsy'. In this poem, rather than a happy-ever-after ending, the princess's decision to stick with her safe but stultifying situation, rather than travel with the gypsies, leaves her broken-hearted.

Frances Cornford is skilled at taking the persona of innocence, such as a princess or a child, in order to explore the complexity of a psychological condition, most commonly regret, grief, alienation and divided duty. It is her treatment of these universal conditions which largely contributes to her appeal. At the same time, the extent to which she can express universal experience is questionable, as it has to be recognised that she was from a comfortably off, upper-middle-class family, and her subjects are often servants, Cambridge gardens and university quadrangles. Siegfried Sassoon identified her gift as this ability to represent universal feeling and her limitation as 'Cambridge intellectualism':

> She succeeds through keeping on her own ground of feeling an experience. She *did* feel and suffer deeply. But it is all overlaid by Cambridge intellectualism and refinement (one might say the same of Virginia Woolf?). It is a cultured humanistic mind speaking, with perfectionist versecraft. The power and the glory of spiritual aspiration are absent. Thoughts and emotions beautifully, sometimes poignantly, articulated. But never 'the roll, the rise, the carol, the creation'. Much as I admired her, I did feel that she was too intense, analytic and cultured for me. That vibrant voice of hers had a quality of academic aloofness about it. One couldn't imagine her outside of Cambridge.[25]

It is true that the culture of the economically comfortable is represented in some of the idioms and diction like 'tucked-up children' and 'bread-and-butter tea' or the allusions to dressing-up and dinner parties. Virginia Woolf found that Frances Cornford's poems struck a chord with herself, 'a harassed middle-class middle-aged woman ... stepping into Hamleys toyshop and buying presents for nephews and nieces',[26] but at least one reader found the poet's attitude patronising; the anonymous reader sent her a postcard with a parody of 'To a Fat Lady seen from a Train':

> How do you know what I lose or gain
> And what do you know of love?
> O pert brown miss in the railway train
> How do you know what I lose or gain?
> Do five rich publicans languish in vain
> Longing to kiss *your* glove?
> How do you know what I lose or gain,
> And what do you know of love?

The postcard was dated May 1910 and signed 'The FWW' [Fat White Woman].[27]

Throughout her life, Frances Cornford wanted to be disassociated from 'the fat white woman who walked through the field in gloves',[28] and from most of her early work.[29] I do not think, however, that such a poem as 'To a Fat Lady seen from a Train' smacks of social snobbery, even unconscious or unintended, but rather of imaginative activity and an attempt to experiment with rhythm. Although the framework of reference may be a cushioned world, Frances Cornford frequently demythologises the alleged securities of wealth and other idylls. In 'August the Thirteenth', for example, what to the outsider would appear to be 'seemly' at The Mount, Marsden, Bucks, is a clockwork routine which is stifling. Again, recourse to the journals and Gwen Raverat's *Period Piece: A Cambridge Childhood* tells us that the two girls were not at ease with the social conventions of their childhood. For them, it was 'torture' to dress up properly, and they dreaded dancing classes, 'the worst of social events'.[30] Although they were more exposed to ethics than dogmas, from *Period Piece* we get a sense of mixed feelings towards their backgrounds. The large family must have provided scope for breadth of outlooks, but Gwen and Frances were evidently independent spirits who had to work through for themselves the questions of duty, religion and convention. It is interesting that a reviewer of the early poems identified the tone of a 'rebellious protest against an unjust world'.[31] Although it cannot be claimed that Frances Cornford was political in any actively socialist sense, she speaks in the language of democracy. The most direct suggestion of an opinion on current events is 'Hitler's face and falling lock' in 'The Granite Fireplace'.

It was the voice of the under-represented that Frances Cornford often aimed to represent. In 'Notes for a Talk' she records that she wanted to show what it feels like to be old, a child or an animal.[32] She was also haunted by the paradox that isolation is the most shared feature of the human condition. Shared isolation is, of course, the essence of two popular poems, 'Epitaph for Everyman' and 'Soldiers on the Platform'. Often, it is the consciousness of death which constitutes that isolation, and yet, paradoxically, Death is also the leveller of social differences. In 'The Trumpet Shall Sound', for example, it is the place where 'Lords and Commons ever equal are'. It is perhaps because they reach beyond her personal context that her poems about death, and especially her poems of the Second World War – when class distinctions were temporarily suspended – are particularly successful. Nearly all of *Travelling Home* (1948) is included in *Collected Poems*. It contains 'Summer Beach', which takes an image common to all age and social groups and depicts bucket-and-spade activity as a metaphor for eking out one's days until death.

Frances Cornford believed in universal experience, which it was the job of the poet to represent: 'I thought the poet's vision always incorporated the general in the particular, and this above all means the images, often concrete images'.[33] She was keen that poetry should not be the property of the élite – 'Do not think of verse writing as a sacred mystery'[34] – and she used forms like ballad, epitaph and epigram which cross cultural delineations. In an article, 'Poetry Readings' for the *Cambridge Review* (1943), she was pleased to observe an increase of attendance at poetry readings because it demonstrated a 'remarkable proof of how much poetry means to an average English audience'.[35] She herself was committed to giving readings because she believed in the need to hear poetry in order to appreciate it. It has to be said, however, that in the literary papers, there are notes for a talk at Foyles, a reading at the Cambridge Literary Circle and a lecture in Edinburgh, rather than records of common-place venues. Incidentally, all these papers include similar points about the climate of poetry in which she grew up and that she found T. S. Eliot 'joyful liberation' from 'moribund clichés'.

As a translator, Frances Cornford was highly respected. Not only did Stephen Spender acknowledge her part in the translation of Chagall, but he also called her 'one of the best translators living'.[36] In her introduction to *Poems from the Russian*, she discusses the processes of translation and declares her intention to compose poetry that works in the translated language and is also faithful to the *spirit* of the original. Esther Polianowsky Salaman was responsible for the literal translation of the Russian language, and Frances Cornford for the reconstruction of the rhythm, mood and the 'psychological forms' of the poetry. She admitted the difficulty of translating images and symbols without losing the essence of the poem.[37]

Many of Frances Cornford's poems are about women, but she was fiercely committed to avoiding subjectivity, partly from the desire to avoid the 'awful word "poetess"' – the concept of which was ridiculed by her sons, who suggested that she entitle her talks on poetry 'lady bard, lady bard, fly away home'.[38] The consistent and vehement eschewal of sentimentality may have started when Christopher advised her to 'wash down the drafted poems with an appropriate strength of de-emotionalising acid' and it became a principle.[39] She criticised Rupert Brooke, for example, for being 'too much a "je" to the end'.[40] In the notes for her *Woman's Hour* talk, she said that poetry 'must cut the umbilical cord between the poem and the writer . . . otherwise it may remain *embarrassingly* personal and emotional.'[41] In this talk, she again states her distaste for her 'frivolous' early poems and addresses the paradox that a writer must draw upon first-hand experience in order to depict the universal. She may well have been influenced by Virginia Woolf in her belief that there are male and female traits in every writer – she admired *A Room of One's Own* and wrote to tell Virginia so; she also told her that she had been 'weeping with delight over *The Common Reader*, and before that, *Mrs Dalloway*'.[42] An admirer, Arthur C. Hervey, however, appreciated the gender-distinctive aspect of Frances Cornford's *Collected Poems*, saying that there should be more poets like herself and Alice Meynell, for 'how can a man have a woman's dreams?' To support the validity of this question, there is an example of when John liked a 'short poem' except for the word 'coloured', which she wanted to keep 'because of the element of hoping phantasy in the woman's mind' (24 March 1932).[43]

Many of her poems, like 'Constant', allude to the altruism and silent grief of women suffering from 'the pain unknown' of loss. 'A Peasant Woman', included in *Twentieth Century Poetry*, edited by Harold Monro,[44] is about the isolation and waiting which such women endure, without regret, at every stage of their lives. 'Mother and Child Asleep' reflects on the requirement of women to give all to their families and then to let them go – 'on that strange morning you must sail alone'. The metaphor of the sailboat is again used in

'The Scholar', referring to the temperamental distance between her husband and his family, and also in a letter where Frances Cornford describes his admirable ability to let his children 'sail away like ships' to independence.[45]

From the Gilbert Murray papers I have learned that after the death of her husband in 1943, in addition to helping Gilbert Murray with a biography of him, she began writing her own memoir, which was never finished; her son Hugh's biography in this book is therefore all the more valuable. An extract from a letter from Lord David Cecil represents something of the enthusiasm generated by readers of Frances Cornford's poetry:

> how much I have enjoyed and admired your new book of poems. I have always loved your poetry, though I have only seen it in occasional anthologies... the beautiful exactness of the observation, the delicate right precision of its phrasing, playing all over them, like sunlight on water... the flicker of your wit and tenderness and sensibility. Not very much poetry written nowadays stirs an answering chord in me, even when I bring myself to admire it. But yours does. Thank you very much.[46]

Further Reading

Anderson, Alan, *A Bibliography of the Writings of Frances Cornford*, Edinburgh, Tragara Press, 1975.

Delaney, Paul, *The Neo-Pagans: Friendship and Love in the Rupert Brooke Circle*, London, Hamish Hamilton, 1987.

Dowson, Jane, 'The Importance of Frances Cornford', *The Charleston Magazine*, Spring 1994, pp.10-14.

—— *Women's Poetry of the 1930s: A Critical Anthology*, London, Routledge, 1996.

Fowler, Helen, chapter on Frances Cornford in *Cambridge Women: Twelve Portraits*, ed. Edward Shils and Carmen Blacker, Cambridge University Press, 1996.

Galassi, Jonathan, ed., *Understand the Weapon, Understand the Wound* [includes some letters of Frances Cornford], Manchester, Carcanet Press, 1976; reprinted as *John Cornford: Collected Writings*, 1986.

Raverat, Gwen, *Period Piece: A Cambridge Childhood*, London, Faber, 1952.

Rogers, Timothy, 'Frances Cornford 1886-1960', *London Magazine*, Vol. 32, Nos. 5-6, Aug./Sept. 1992, pp.101-112.

Notes

1. Frances Cornford saw proofs of *On a Calm Shore* but died before it was published.
2. Harold Monro, *Some Contemporary Poets*, London, Simpkins and Marshall, 1920, p.179.
3. Review of *Best Poems of 1924*, ed. Thomas Moult, *Time and Tide*, 20 March 1925.
4. Editorial, *The Listener*, 7 June 1933.
5. 'L'Etranger', in *The New Statesman and Nation*, 12 October 1924, is one example of a prizewinning poem.
6. Letter from Naomi Mitchison, 16 November 1954, Add. MSS 58421. Unless otherwise stated, all manuscripts are in the Literary Papers of Frances Cornford, Department of Manuscripts, British Library, London.
7. Letter from 'Margaret', The Cottage, Chillington, Kingsbridge, S. Devon. Add. MSS 58421.
8. *The New Statesman and Nation*, 21 November 1942.
9. See Add. MSS 58423.
10. See letter from Thomas Hardy, written from Max Gate, Dorset, and dated Jan. 13, 1910, 'Your father's name is introduction sufficient, and I shall be pleased to see you.'
11. Journal entries 1902 and 1934, Add. MSS 58390.
12. Letter from 'David' – [he had just finished a book on the history of thought] – Add. MSS 58421.
13. 'Views and Recollections of a Sunday Poet', Tuesday, 27 March 1956, Add. MSS 58387.
14. See Galassi, 1976, and Maxwell, D.E.S., 'Christopher Caudwell and John Cornford', *Poets in the Thirties*, London, Routledge & Kegan Paul, 1969.
15. See Preface to *On a Calm Shore*. See also correspondence with Christopher, Add. MSS 58412.
16. Journal notes, Literary Memoirs, Add. MSS 58384.
17. These points are made almost verbatim in her notes for 'Reading at Cambridge Literary Circle', 2 October 1953 and 'Lunchtime Talk at Foyles', Add. MSS 58386.
18. 'Lecture on Poetry', undated, p.22, Add. MSS 58385.
19. Letters to Gilbert Murray, undated, possibly 1956, and October 1948, Gilbert Murray Papers, 113 and 99 respectively, Oxford, Bodleian Library.
20. See 'Aunt Etty', Chapter 3, Raverat, 1952.
21. See journal, 1901, and Letters to Gilbert Murray, 27, Gilbert Murray Papers.
22. See Letters in Add. MSS 58421.
23. Letters, Add. MSS 59421.
24. Ibid.
25. Siegfried Sassoon (1961), in Dame Felicitas Corrigan, *Siegfried Sassoon: A Poet's Pilgrimage*, London, Victor Gollancz, 1973, pp.68-9.
26. Letter from Virginia Woolf, Add. MSS 58422.
27. Add. MSS 58421.

28 'Lunchtime Talk at Foyles', p.1, Add. MSS 58386.

29 Literary Memoirs and Memories, Add. MSS 58384.

30 See Chapters XIII and XIV on 'Clothes' and 'Society' in Raverat, 1952.

31 Review of Poems, *The Times*, June/July 1910, undated cutting in Add. MSS 58421.

32 'Notes for a Talk', Add. MSS 58386.

33 'Notes for a Talk', Add. MSS 58385.

34 'Lecture on Poetry', undated, p.6, Add. MSS 58385.

35 'Poetry Readings', *Cambridge Review*, 20 November 1943.

36 See letter from Stephen Spender to 'My dear Frances', dated Feb. 12 [no year], Add. MSS 58424.

37 See 'Lecture on Translation', undated but probably 1920s, Add. MSS 58385.

38 See 'Views and Recollections of a Sunday Poet', Add. MSS 58387.

39 Letter from Christopher, Add. MSS 58412.

40 'Views and Recollections of a Sunday Poet', Add. MSS 58387.

41 'Guest of the Week', *Woman's Hour*, BBC, 4 November 1959, Add. MSS 58387.

42 Letter to Virginia Woolf, 1 February 1926. Sussex Papers.

43 See Jonathan Galassi, 1976, p.146.

44 *Twentieth Century Poetry*, ed. Harold Monro, 1929; revised and enlarged by Alida Monro, London, Chatto & Windus, 1933.

45 Letter to Gilbert Murray, 24 March 1943, Gilbert Murray papers, 95.

46 Letter from Lord David Cecil to Frances Cornford, Add. MSS 58423.

The Cornford family in 1928

Back Row: Helena, John
Middle Row: Clare, Francis, Frances, Christopher
                       Hugh

Frances Cornford 1886–1960
Hugh Cornford

What I have written is a cross between a memoir and a short life. My mother was born in Cambridge on 30 March 1886. Her life was divided by three long episodes of severe depression, with a further recurrence in the months before she died. It seems probable that she inherited this tendency to depression from both parents. Her father was Francis Darwin, son of Charles Darwin, and her mother his second wife Ellen (née Crofts). She had a half-brother, Bernard, whose mother Amy Ruck died when he was born. Francis Darwin acted for a time as assistant and secretary to his own father and he later moved to Cambridge, where he had been an undergraduate at Trinity College; he became a Lecturer and then Reader in Botany.

Francis Darwin was, by all accounts, the most charming and cultivated of his distinguished brothers and sisters. He played several musical instruments and wrote humorous essays. He shared with the others an enquiring mind, absolute integrity, a lack of self-consciousness and a certain innocence. He seems to have suffered from bouts of depression when young and certainly did in later life. This was doubtless partly due to the tragic death of his first wife in childbirth, but there does seem to have been an inherent melancholic tendency as well.

Ellen Crofts came from a north country family and was a great-niece of William Wordsworth. She was an early fellow and a college lecturer in English at Newnham College, Cambridge. Although Frances was very close to her, and her first serious 'nervous breakdown' followed closely on her mother's death at the age of forty-eight, Frances rarely talked about her. No portraits and few photographs survive. I know far more about her from her niece Gwen Raverat's (née Darwin) autobiography, *Period Piece: A Cambridge Childhood*. To Gwen, Ellen seemed 'wonderfully up-to-date and literary'. She had her rough black hair cut unconventionally short and she and her friends '*smoked cigarettes*'. Interestingly, Gwen records, 'It is odd how little I remember Aunt Ellen, though I was eighteen when she died' and later, 'Aunt Ellen was not a happy person though I don't know what was wrong'. Finally, she quotes Jane Harrison, distinguished classical scholar, contemporary and close friend of Ellen at Newnham, as saying long after her death, ' "I could not be sorry when Ellen died, because she was so unhappy: though I don't know why. She loved her husband and her child and had everything she wanted in the world. Was it a temperamental melancholy; had she a real distaste for life?" [1]

Frances had a secure childhood in a comfortable upper-middle-class home. Her half-brother Bernard, with whom she got on very well, was nine years older than her and she had a number of intelligent and compatible first cousins living within walking distance in Cambridge – the sons and daughters of her father's brothers George and Horace Darwin. All the male cousins and some of the girls went on to preparatory and then public schools (Bernard was at Eton). Frances always maintained that she was not educated, as she neither went to school nor a university, but was taught at home, partly by her governess Ada Sharpley 'who made so much of the poetry in my childhood'. [2] Some classes were held jointly with the cousins. She was taught drawing by a Miss Greene, who was an aunt of Graham Greene. Her mother read poetry to her at an early age – especially Elizabethan and seventeenth-century lyrics. Her French was good and she had some grounding in Latin, but none in Greek. She enjoyed geometry, but alleged that the rest of mathematics remained a mystery. One advantage of this private education was that she was never inculcated with the empire-building and flag-wagging ethic then current at boys' public schools, and probably to a lesser extent at girls' schools too.

Both Frances' parents were agnostics and she had no formal religious instruction – one governess was rebuked for reading the Bible to her. She was not christened as a child, unlike the other cousins; at first she accepted this and there is a drawing of her in Gwen Raverat's *Period Piece*, depicting her at nine years old telling Gwen, aged ten, that 'it was not at all the thing nowadays to believe in Christianity any more. It simply was not done'. [3] Later in childhood and adolescence Frances was assailed by doubts, and gradually over the years she was converted to Christianity; she was christened into the Church of England in 1924 and confirmed in the same year. I think it was in that year that all five of us children were christened as a job lot. We attended services on Sunday mornings at the nearby village of Madingley in the late 1920s and early 1930s. In later life Frances became a regular member of the congregation at St Benet's Church in Cambridge. My father, although the son of an Anglican clergyman, had been an agnostic since first coming up to Cambridge as an undergraduate. As a relatively young fellow of Trinity College he made a major contribution to the abolition of compulsory chapel in the college.

The death of her mother in 1903 was a shattering blow and precipitated the first of her major depressions. Speaking as a doctor,

I believe that Frances suffered from recurrent depression or depressive psychosis. This is not just a reaction to some distressing circumstance; it can arise without an obvious cause, as it is a disturbance of the chemistry of part of the brain. In this instance, as may happen, there was an event which triggered it and possibly there was an associated hormonal cause as in the two subsequent depressions: a late onset of her periods, childbirth and the menopause. There was no specific treatment for this sort of depression – known as Cyclothymia – in those days. This first episode lasted for over three years, some of which she spent in Switzerland. Her eventual recovery over three to four weeks was sudden and dramatic. She returned home to her father in Cambridge with renewed energy and vitality.

During the years at home after her recovery, she painted, led an active social life and started to write. I cannot better her own description of how she came to publish poems:

> I gave no consideration to the verse I found myself writing from time to time because the whole ambition of my life was to be a painter... The painter William Rothenstein was a friend of my parents, always very kind to me, interested and helpful, though at the same time never falsely encouraging. When I was a grown-up young woman I used sometimes to sit and draw with him in his studio, and he would talk to me about anything that came into his head. One day agreeing with something or other he had said, I added: 'I've written a poem about that'. Afterwards he made me produce a few youthful lyrics from the bottom of my writing case, and then said 'But this is what you ought to do'. Those eight words opened my eyes. Though I realised that he had overpraised what I had actually shown him I saw from then on that verses came naturally and that painting did not.[4]

She goes on to say that Rothenstein persuaded her father to print privately her first volume of poems (*Poems*, 1910) and that this was received with some critical acclaim.

No account of my mother or her relationship with my father can omit reference to Jane Harrison. As a close friend and colleague of her mother, Frances had known her all her life. Jane was a brilliant scholar and teacher. She was handsome with a striking and fascinating personality. She was one of the first scholars to apply anthropology to the interpretation of Greek religion. She, together with my father and Gilbert Murray, later became known collectively as The Cambridge Ritualists. They sought the ritual and social origins of

Greek religion, philosophy and literature and caused an upheaval in conventional classical studies. In 1908 Jane Harrison introduced Frances to Francis Cornford, with whom she had also developed a close friendship, and with whom she was probably in love, although he was twenty-five years younger. He had recently published his immortal satire on university politics, *Microcosmographia Academica*, and my mother was anxious to meet the then-anonymous author. Soon they were seeing each other fairly often and Jane Harrison seemed to wish to throw them together. My father was actually escorting Jane to Devon to convalesce from an operation when my parents became engaged by letter. Frances was in Belfast acting as hostess for her father, who was then President of the British Association for the Advancement of Science. Frances married Francis in 1909. As a wedding present her father built them a large house in about an acre of ground two miles from the centre of Cambridge, Conduit Head. They had a cook and other resident domestic help. Frances always maintained that she disliked the responsibilities of being grown up and that she had never wanted to run a house.

One event of lasting significance to my parents and their contemporaries was a production of the masque *Comus* in 1908, the year before their wedding. This was organised by Justin Brooke, founder of The Marlowe Society, and Rupert Brooke (no relation to Justin) in order to celebrate the tercentenary of Milton's birth. Rupert Brooke directed and acted as The Attendant Spirit. As the performance took place out of term, women were allowed to play the female parts. They were mainly recruited by Jane Harrison from students at Newnham. Francis Cornford, who had attended rehearsals, was pressed at 'the great age' of thirty-three to take the part of Comus because of his powers of speaking verse; Frances and Gwen Darwin designed the costumes. On the evening of the performance my mother saw my father lying back in a chair to be made up, and she had a sudden premonition that she would see his face in death. This came back to her as he lay back on his pillows the day he died thirty-four years later.

After *Comus*, Frances became an intimate friend and confidante of Rupert Brooke, as she was to a lesser extent of others in the group sometimes loosely described as The Neo-Pagans: Justin Brooke, Jacques and Gwen Raverat, Ka Cox and others. Rupert felt that he could trust Frances as she was happily married. He told her of his incredibly complicated, neurotic and largely unhappy love affairs with Ka Cox, Bryn and Noel Olivier and Cathleen Nesbitt. She listened and offered him sensible advice, such as, after the end of his affair with Ka Cox, that he should go abroad for at least a year and do hard physical work until he was so tired at night that he could only just crawl to bed and sleep. As far back as 1907 or 1908, she wrote the poem 'Youth', describing him as 'A young Apollo, golden-haired', a portrait which he disliked. They discussed their poems, but sometimes he mocked her verse, gently to her face, but more savagely behind her back, for what he considered to be her 'heart cry' poetry. She was very fond of him but thought him neurotic and drifting. They met in London and said an affectionate farewell shortly before he set off for the Dardanelles and his early death. She felt that they both had a premonition that they would not meet again.

My parents had different but complementary characters. My father was introverted, reserved and practical. He was a distinguished classical scholar, successively Lecturer and Reader in Greek and finally Professor of Ancient Philosophy. He had little or no small talk and was often silent in company, as my mother recorded in 'The Scholar', written some years after his death:

> You often went to breathe a timeless air
> And walk with those you love, perhaps the most.
> You spoke to Plato. You were native there

He once wrote of himself that he had spent much of his life in Athens in the 4th and 5th centuries BC. This was queried by the printers' proof-reader! If he wanted to go back to his study and his work he had the ability to abstract himself from a conversation and to leave the room without anyone noticing.

Frances was an extrovert and got on easily with people. She had great gifts as a conversationalist and could make any subject seem interesting. She did not dominate a conversation but put people at their ease and got them to talk. When visiting scholars came to see my father he would say to her 'Come and start us off'. She would and did and then discreetly withdrew. She wrote letters to a variety of correspondents and a variety of people came to see her, often for advice. Every Sunday during the university term there was open house for tea. This was for pupils of my father and any friends who cared to drop in. I remember these occasions with pleasure, as often undergraduates would play with us. Astutely and typically, my mother noticed that the women students did not join in. She thought that they assumed, perhaps subconsciously, that many years of this kind of thing lay ahead of them. For some years an amateur choral group, known as 'The Corncrakes', met roughly once a week in our house and gave a concert in the summer.

My parents were devoted to each other and both must have suffered during Frances' depressions. One lasted two years after Christopher was born in 1917, only a year after John, and the other lasted six years from 1934 to 1940. Throughout both depressions Francis remained considerate, patient and supportive and also optimistic about her eventual recovery. Although he had the support of nurses, governesses and domestic help, he was not temperamentally suited to being a 'single parent'; all five children adored him, as he did us, but he did not find it easy to be on really intimate terms with growing children.

I believe that her recovery from her second depression was less dramatic and not as complete as that from her first. I was born in 1921 and my younger sister Clare in 1924. Frances said that she always felt very well when pregnant but she was inclined to depression when breast-feeding. In Christopher's words, during the 1920s and early 1930s she was 'invalidish'. She seemed always to be in need of a lot of rest, had a special diet and used to go off for consultations in London. I gradually came to realise that she was different from other mothers and that she was 'delicate'. She may have inherited some of the Darwin hypochondria – even when well she never went away for a night without packing a thermometer – but I do not believe that her lack of energy and robustness was all psychosomatic.

All of us were sent to boarding schools at roughly the age of nine. I suppose it was usual in upper-middle-class families at the time but now I wonder if it was not done partly because of Frances' invalidism – to lessen the strain and the actual number of people in the house. Despite this invalidism she was effectively the centre of family life. Her relationship with her sons was easier than with her daughters. Helena was born in 1913, then John (1916) and Christopher (1917) were born in close succession. This was followed by my mother's second depression and two years away from home. Helena seemed to think that Frances did not love her and this made for difficulties in their relationship. In later years Frances admired her poetry and achievements as a ballet dancer. Clare was ten when Frances' longest and worst depression (1934–40) began and their former closeness was not resumed until the last years of my mother's life. Before that they tended to be rather critical of each other.

With John, however, there was a strong bond through poetry, especially in his adolescence. Both parents had an immense admiration for his intellectual power and his voracious reading habits. There is a remarkable correspondence between Frances and John written during his sixth form years at Stowe.[5] He was often a ferocious critic of her work but Frances never took offence, always replied in detail and always encouraged him. The correspondence also shows his growing preoccupation with Marxism and gradual conversion to Communism. My parents were dismayed by his, for the time, unconventional private life. During university vacations he lived with his girlfriend, Ray Peters, quite openly in Cambridge. John was a determined person and they wisely let him go his own way. Their differences in no way diminished my parents' admiration or affection for him. Christopher always had a harmonious, if not entirely uncritical, relationship with Frances. I quote from something he said about her to a friend who was writing an article about her: 'My mother was extraordinary in that whenever she came into the room everything seemed more interesting and exciting... She made us feel valued and made us feel as though we were somebody and took a great interest in anything we wrote or drew or made. Somehow one felt enhanced by her, at least I did'. I would endorse my brother Christopher's recollection; I too felt that when a child I could ask or tell her anything.

Her major depression began in midsummer 1934. She was away in various nursing homes until January 1937, when we got the tragic news of John's death on his twenty-first birthday fighting with the International Brigade on the republican side in the Spanish Civil War. She returned home then, still obviously deeply depressed. She told me later that the worst feature of her long illness was that she felt numb inside, could not grieve for John and felt no emotion on seeing her other children again after so long. She was alarmingly thin, looked much older, and her voice had a curious plaintive quality. For the next three-and-a-half years she lived an invalid life; she spent almost all day long lying on her bed in ill-fitting clothes in nondescript shades of brown and only came downstairs at tea time. She wrote almost no poetry but continued a desultory correspondence with some very old friends. Towards the end of this time she was also able to help my father who was translating Plato's *Republic*; each day he would read aloud what he had done and this routine continued after her recovery. The dedication of the translation reads, 'To F.C.C. in gratitude for many hours patiently given to the amendment of this version by one whose sense of good English is a never failing guide... F.M.C.'. Her recovery from this depression was as dramatic as that from the first. It coincided roughly with the German invasion of Norway and the fall of France. From that time on the days of having two or three resident domestic helps were over; the younger ones volunteered or were conscripted into some form of war service. The next nineteen years were active, energetic and productive ones for my mother. My father, however, lived only another three years, but Frances seemed to have been prepared for his death from pneumonia in January 1943; although she was very upset, this did not trigger another depression as we all feared.

Since 1937 Francis had been the treasurer of a hostel for Spanish refugee children – mainly Basques. At first they were in a huge former country rectory and were educated there. About a year after the war began it was decided that they should be boarded out with Cambridge families and go to local schools. With some help Frances continued the work for many years. She kept in touch with the families, often bicycling to the far side of Cambridge, dealt with crises, and gave an annual tea party for them all. Frances also quite often had people we called her 'lame ducks' in tow. I remember them as mainly single ladies with literary ambitions and sad personal lives.

A matter much on her mind when she was ill and after she had recovered was to get in touch with John's son James.[6] When John was killed in Spain his great friend at Cambridge, an American millionaire, Michael Straight, offered to subsidise James's education and furthermore found employment for his mother Ray Peters on the Dartington Hall Estate in Devon. Dartington Hall had been founded by Michael's mother, Dorothy Elmhirst, and her second husband Leonard. Francis and Frances had made several visits to the Elmhirsts, who were charming and generous people. Incidentally it was here that Frances met Stephen and Natasha Spender, a meeting which led to a fruitful collaboration with Stephen and a life-long friendship with Natasha. During the war Michael Straight was unable to send money from the U.S.A. and James's education was being paid for by the Elmhirsts. James was a boarder at Dartington School from the age of three and lived in Totnes during the holidays. Frances succeeded in making contact with James and his mother, and was anxious to integrate James into the Cornford family. By 1943, she had, as it were, opened negotiations to change his surname to Cornford, to adopt him and for him to come and live with her in Cambridge; she arranged for him to go to a local preparatory school and later to Winchester College, *and* for Michael Straight and the Elmhirsts to continue to subsidise him. As the Elmhirsts had founded one of the most progressive schools in this country, this is evidence both of their generosity and of her tendency to manipulate. When James came to Cambridge on a permanent basis in 1944, at the age of eight, Frances was fifty-eight and her youngest child, Clare, was twenty.

After 1940, Frances had resumed writing poetry and produced a further volume of poems, *Travelling Home* (1948) and a translation of Russian verse, *Poems from the Russian* (1943) with Esther Salaman. During the war we shared our house with Esther Salaman, her husband Myer and their children – one roof but separate accommodation. Esther was Russian and gave Frances a literal translation and then read her the poem in Russian several times over. She then produced an English version. Like her other translations these were well received. She also published a translation of the *Dur Désir de Durer* by Marc Chagall, jointly with Stephen Spender, who described her as 'one of the best translators living'.

In 1954 Frances Cornford published her *Collected Poems*, which were in fact her selected poems – 'all the poems I wish to preserve from my previously published work'. She relied to a large extent on the advice of John Hayward at the Cresset Press. He was a considerable figure in the literary world and a close friend of T. S. Eliot. He had a form of muscular dystrophy which confined him to a wheelchair. This also affected the muscles of his face and gave him a distorted appearance with large slack lips. He was embittered, extremely amusing and could be malicious, although never towards Frances, as far as I know. I do not think that he greatly influenced her choice of poems but he did persuade her to amend them in ways which did not always improve them. He temporarily replaced her gentler mentor Sir Edward ('Eddie') Marsh.

Although she was never part of literary or artistic circles, Frances had several friends from among them. Max Beerbohm and Will Rothenstein were friends of her father and used to stay with them. She remained on affectionate terms with the Rothenstein family. At different times she was on friendly, but never on close, terms with Walter de la Mare (whom she greatly admired), Eric Gill, Bertrand Russell, Siegfried Sassoon, Ralph and Ursula Vaughan Williams, Lawrence Whistler and Virginia Woolf. Christopher Hassall was a close friend and confidant.

Frances always stayed up until everyone else had gone to bed and this is when she worked on her poems. The first versions were often on the back of envelopes or odd scraps of paper, often with suggestions for alternative lines, phrases or words. She would show these to whoever was in the house the following day, seeking their preferences and comments. She sometimes accepted these and sometimes not. She was aware of having a high degree of professionalism and expertise as a poet and could not bear to be called a 'poetess'. Despite this I do not think of her as being a feminist in any militant sense. I know that she was well aware of the nature of women's lives and problems, their often subservient role and frustrated ambitions, and she and my father went to meetings in Cambridge to support women's suffrage before the First World War. Frances was not greatly interested in day to day politics and would describe herself as liberal with a small 'l'. She once told me that she would prefer to be taken in to dinner by Mr Macmillan than by Mr Gaitskell.

In 1953 she decided that the family home, Conduit Head, was too big for her and that she was tired of having to let out part of the house. Her declared intention was to find a detached house with a garden in a quiet situation near the centre of Cambridge. When she found that this was not possible she chose a large semi-detached house about a mile from the centre. She had it altered and re-decorated and made it into a very pleasant and comfortable house. She became more hospitable than ever with a specially warm welcome for grandchildren, and held regular coffee evenings for students.

It is very difficult to judge objectively about the appearance of one's mother. Judging by photographs I think it is fair to say that she was a striking and handsome child. As a young woman I would say again that she was striking and attractive rather than beautiful. Her skin was curiously dark which gave her a gypsy-like look. Relatively early in life, as she herself ruefully remarked, she became 'slashed with wrinkles' – possibly this was due to her passion for being in the sun. She was distinguished in old age and her black hair had scarcely a grey strand in all her seventy-four years.

In February or March 1960 she had a heart attack. At first she seemed to make a reasonable recovery but she developed chronic heart failure that did not respond well to treatment. She became generally unwell, tired and unhungry and in the early summer her depression returned and deepened. Her last months were sad as her vitality slowly drained away.

I realise that I have been critical in places. It is true that my mother could be mildly exasperating and manipulative at times. The picture I would like to leave, however, is of someone warm, courageous, generous, affectionate and enormous fun to be with. It seems appropriate to finish with her poem 'Epitaph for Everyman'.

Although perhaps harsh on herself, it indicates her insight into human nature and I have no doubt that she thought that it also applied to her:

> My heart was more disgraceful, more alone,
> And more courageous than the world has known.
>
> O passer-by, my heart was like your own.

Notes

1 Gwen Raverat, *Period Piece: A Cambridge Childhood*, dedicated 'to Frances', London, Faber, (1952) 1958, pp.192-5; 219.
2 Frances Cornford, dedication to *Travelling Home* (1948).
3 Raverat, 1958, pp.219-20.
4 'Frances Cornford Writes', *Poetry Book Society Bulletin*, No. 3, September 1954.
5 See Jonathan Galassi, ed., *John Cornford: Collected Writings*, Manchester, Carcanet Press, 1986.
6 James had been born to John and his girlfriend Ray Peters in 1936, shortly before John's death.

AUTUMN MORNING AT CAMBRIDGE

I ran out in the morning, when the air was clean and new
And all the grass was glittering and grey with autumn dew,
I ran out to an apple-tree and pulled an apple down,
And all the bells were ringing in the old grey town.

Down in the town off the bridges and the grass,
They are sweeping up the leaves to let the people pass,
Sweeping up the old leaves, golden-reds and browns,
Whilst the men go to lecture with the wind in their gowns.

October 1902

THE WATCH

I wakened on my hot, hard bed,
Upon the pillow lay my head;
Beneath the pillow I could hear
My little watch was ticking clear.
I thought the throbbing of it went
Like my continual discontent;
I thought it said in every tick:
I am so sick, so sick, so sick;
O Death, come quick, come quick, come quick,
Come quick, come quick, come quick, come quick.

PRE-EXISTENCE

I laid me down upon the shore
    And dreamed a little space;
I heard the great waves break and roar
    The sun was on my face.

My idle hands and fingers brown
    Played with the pebbles grey;
The waves came up, the waves went down,
    Both thundering and gay.

The pebbles smooth and salt and round
    Were warm upon my hands,
Like little people I had found
    Sitting among the sands.

The grains of sand completely small
    Soft through my fingers ran;
The sun shone down upon us all,
    And so my dream began:

How all of this had been before,
    How ages far away
I lay on some forgotten shore
    As here I lie today.

The waves came shining up the sands,
    As here today they shine;
And in my pre-Pelasgian hands
    The sand was warm and fine.

I have forgotten whence I came
    Or where my home might be,
Or by what strange and savage name
    I called that thundering sea.

I only know the sun shone down
    As still it shines today,
And friendly in my fingers brown
    The little pebbles lay.

1907

2

LONDON STREETS
Villanelle

'The blundering and cruel ways of nature'
                                        CHARLES DARWIN

O Providence, I will not praise,
Neither for fear nor joy of gain,
Your blundering and cruel ways.

This city where the dun fog stays,
These tired faces in the rain,
O Providence, I will not praise.

Here in the mud and wind that slays
In the cold streets, I scan again
Your blundering and cruel ways.

And all men's miserable days,
And all their ugliness and pain,
O Providence, I will not praise.

I will not join the hymns men raise
Like slaves who would avert, in vain,
Your blundering and cruel ways.

At least, in this distracted maze,
I love the truth and see it plain;
O Providence, I will not praise
Your blundering and cruel ways.

    1908

YOUTH

A young Apollo, golden-haired,
  Stands dreaming on the verge of strife.
Magnificently unprepared
  For the long littleness of life.

TO A FAT LADY SEEN FROM A TRAIN

O why do you walk through the fields in gloves,
        Missing so much and so much?
O fat white woman whom nobody loves,
        Why do you walk through the fields in gloves,
When the grass is soft as the breast of doves
        And shivering-sweet to the touch?
O why do you walk through the fields in gloves,
        Missing so much and so much?

A RECOLLECTION

My father's friend came once to tea.
He laughed and talked. He spoke to me.
But in another week they said
That friendly pink-faced man was dead.

'How sad...' they said, 'the best of men...'
So I said too, 'How sad'; but then
Deep in my heart I thought, with pride,
'I know a person who has died'.

A WASTED DAY

I spoiled the day;
Hotly, in haste,
All the calm hours
I gashed and defaced.

Let me forget,
Let me embark,
Sleep for my boat,
And sail through the dark.

Till a new day
Heaven shall send
Whole as an apple,
And kind as a friend.

IN DORSET

From muddy road to muddy lane
I plodded through the falling rain;
For miles and miles was nothing there
But mist, and mud, and hedges bare.

At length approaching I espied
Two gypsy women side by side;
They turned their faces broad and bold
And brown and freshened by the cold,
And stared at me in gypsy wise
With shrewd, unfriendly, savage eyes.

No word they said, no more dared I,
And so we passed each other by,
The only living things that met
In all those miles of mist and wet.

5

AUTUMN MIDNIGHT

Why is it grown so suddenly cold at night?
The handles of the chest-of-drawers are bright
And round, and hard, and like a usurer's eyes –
Perhaps it is the moon's cold from the skies?
I wish I had not woken thus alone –
I think she pours a coldness of her own
On each loved leaf upon the garden trees,
So that they never can recover. These
And ruined starry daisies all will say:
'Queen of the garden, now we go away,
Now we have known the cold of the moon that kills
And though tomorrow all the heaven fills
With golden light until the chill sun's set,
Though for an hour the midges minuet,
Though for an hour we glisten in the sun,
Our day, our day is done.'

I'll sleep again in this warm cave of bed;
Tomorrow all the flowers will be dead.

THE NEW-BORN BABY'S SONG

When I was twenty inches long,
I could not hear the thrushes' song;
The radiance of morning skies
Was most displeasing to my eyes.

For loving looks, caressing words,
I cared no more than sun or birds;
But I could bite my mother's breast,
And that made up for all the rest.

THE COUNTRY BEDROOM

My room's a square and candle-lighted boat,
In the surrounding depths of night afloat;
My windows are the portholes and the seas
The sound of rain on the dark apple-trees.

Seamonster-like beneath, an old horse blows
A snort of darkness from his sleeping nose,
Below, among drowned daisies. Far off, hark!
Far off one owl amidst the waves of dark.

THE PRINCESS AND THE GYPSIES

As I looked out one May morning
    I saw the tree-tops green;
I said: 'My crown I will lay down
    And live no more a queen.'

Then I tripped down my golden steps
    Dressed in my silken gown,
And when I stood in the open wood
    I met some gypsies brown.

'O gentle, gentle gypsies
    That roam the wide world through,
Because I hate my crown and state,
    O let me come with you!

'My councillors are old and grey
    And sit in narrow chairs,
But you can hear the birds sing clear
    And your hearts are as light as theirs.'

'If you would come along with us
    Then you must count the cost,
For though in Spring the sweet birds sing,
    In Winter comes the frost.

'Your ladies serve you all the day
    With courtesy and care,
Your fine-shod feet they tread so neat
    But a gypsy's feet go bare.

'You wash in water running warm
    Through basins all of gold;
The streams where we roam have silvery foam,
    But the streams, the streams are cold.

'And barley bread is bitter to taste,
    Whilst sugary cakes they please.
Which will you choose, O which will you choose,
    Which will you choose of these?

'For if you choose the mountain streams
    And barley bread to eat,
Your heart will be free as the birds in the tree
    But the stones will cut your feet.

'The mud will spoil your silken gown
    And stain your insteps high,
The dogs in the farm will wish you harm
    And bark as you go by.

'And though your heart grow deep and gay
    Your heart grow wise and rich,
The cold will make your bones to ache
    And you will die in a ditch.'

'O gentle, gentle gypsies
    That roam the wide world through,
Although I praise your wandering ways
    I dare not come with you.'

I hung about their fingers brown
    My ruby rings and chain,
And with my head as heavy as lead
    Turned me back again.

As I went up the palace steps
    I heard the gypsies laugh;
The birds of spring so sweet did sing,
    It broke my heart in half.

SUSAN TO DIANA
Villanelle

Your youth is like a water-wetted stone,
A pebble by the living sea made rare,
Bright with a beauty that is not its own.

Behold it flushed like flowers newly-blown,
Miraculously fresh beyond compare,
Your youth is like a water-wetted stone.

For when the triumphing tide recedes, alone
The stone will stay, and shine no longer there
Bright with a beauty that is not its own.

But lie and dry as joyless as a bone,
Because the sorceress sea has gone elsewhere.
Your youth is like a water-wetted stone.

Then all your lovers will be children, shown
Their treasure only transitory-fair,
Bright with a beauty that is not its own.

Remember this before your hour is flown;
O you, who are so glorious, beware!
Your youth is like a water-wetted stone,
Bright with a beauty that is not its own.

A LODGING FOR THE NIGHT
[original title 'The Old Nurse']

I am an old woman, comfortable, calm and wise
Often I see the spirits of the dead with my own eyes.
They come into my house. I am no more afraid
Than of the coal-scuttle or my breakfast newly laid.
One night over the fields the wind blew wild,
And I thought I heard in it the ravaging voice of a child.
I thought I heard in it, sweeping the cold lands,
The voice of a child who suddenly misses those only hands
That understood to make him safe, usual, and warm.
It cried unceasingly until I knew it was not the voice of the storm.
I tried to fall asleep; but how could I sleep,
And hear that creature in despair continually weep?
Then to the grown spirits imploringly I said:
'Friends give me here that new spirit who is lately dead,
Who will not enter your new world of light
Because he misses the hands of his mother this first night,
And she, poor soul, lies weeping tear on tear
And cannot pierce the night with love. But I hear.
Give me her wandering child!' Then, as I lay in bed,
Against my breast I felt a small and blunt-nosed head,
A cold sob-quivering body growing calm
And toes like round cold buds that warmed inside my palm.
Soon in the hushing night and darkness deep,
That comforted safe spirit sighed and fell asleep,
And I slept too, most satisfied, until
I woke and saw to-morrow's dawn, everywhere cold and still.
But out of my white bed where morning shone
Out of my arms, away, the new-born spirit gone.

CONTEMPORARIES
[original title 'No Immortality']

Can it be possible when we grow old
And Time destroys us, that your image too,
The timeless beauty that your youth bestowed
(As though you'd lain a moment since by the river
Thinking and dreaming under the grey sky
When May was in the hedges) will dissolve?
This unique image now we hold: your smile,
Which kept a secret sweetness like a child's
Though you might be most sad, your frowning eyes,
Can they be drowned in Time, and nothing left
To the revolving hard, enamelled world
Full, full forever of fresh fears and births
And busyness, of all you were? Perhaps
A thousand years ago some Greek boy died
So lovely-bodied, so adored, so young,
Like us, his lovers treasured senseless things,
And laughed with tears remembering his laughter,
And there was friendship in the very sound
Of his forgotten name to them. Of him
Now we know nothing, nothing is altered now
Because of all he was. Most loved, on you
Can such oblivion fall? Then, if it can,
How futile, how absurd the life of man.

April 1915

APARTMENTS

Now the forgiving sun, with beams aslope,
Who, in pure sky where not a chimney smokes,
Rose over green, umbrageous, rooted oaks,
Enters the city room, that has no pride,
Goldenly, with fresh morning airs allied,
And to the blistered washing-stand says: Hope.

11

THE OLD FRIEND

[original title 'The Dead One']

The wrong you did is gentle, like the trust
                You put in us, and like your voice and air,
The wrong you have done is very quiet, just
                Not being there.

CAMBRIDGESHIRE

The stacks, like blunt impassive temples, rise
Across flat fields against the autumnal skies.
The hairy-footed horses plough the land,
Or as in prayer and meditation stand
Upholding square, primeval, dung-stained carts,
With an unending patience in their hearts.

Nothing is changed. The farmer's gig goes by
Against the horizon. Surely, the same sky,
So vast and yet familiar, grey and mild,
And streaked with light like music, I, a child,
Lifted my face from leaf-edged lanes to see,
Late-coming home, to bread-and-butter tea.

12

AT THE END

The day my great-aunt Sarah died, how I remember well,
She lay alone with daffodils and never rang her bell.
She lay as quiet as her chair and books upon her shelf.
She gave no trouble to her nurse, no trouble to herself.
She was more quiet than the bare, ploughed fields that lay outside.
The knowledge in her listening face as certain was, and wide.

A GLIMPSE

O grasses wet with dew, yellow fallen leaves,
Smooth-shadowed waters Milton loved, green banks,
Arched bridges, rooks, and rain-leaved willow-trees,
Stone, serious familiar colleges,
Cambridge, my home:
The figure of a scholar carrying back
Books to the library, absorbed, content,
Seeming as everlasting as the elms
Bark-wrinkled, puddled round their roots, the bells,
And the far shouting in the football fields.

The same since I was born, the same to be
When all my children's children grow old men.

FÉRI BEKASSY★
[original title 'Féri Dead']

We, who must grow old and staid,
Full of wisdom, much afraid,
In our hearts like flowers keep
Love for you until we sleep.

You the brave, and you the young
You of a thousand songs unsung,
Burning brain, and ardent word,
You the lovely and absurd.

Say, on that Galician plain
Are you arguing again?
Does a trench or ruined tree
Hear your – 'O, I *don't* agree!'

We, who must grow staid and old,
Full of caution, worn and cold,
In our hearts, like flowers keep
Your image, till we also sleep.

1915

**THE WOMAN WITH THE BABY
TO THE PHILOSOPHERS**

How can I dread you, O portentous wise,
When I consider you were once this size?
How cringe before the sage who understands,
Who once had foolish, perfect, waving hands,
As small as these are? How bow down in dread,
When I conceive your warm, domed, downy head
Smelling of soap? O you – from North to South
Renowned – who put your toes inside your mouth.

★ Férencz Bekassy (1891-1915): Hungarian poet, scholar of King's College,
Cambridge, killed in action on the Eastern Front, 1915.

SHE WARNS HIM

I am a lamp, a lamp that is out;
  I am a shallow stream;
In it are neither pearls or trout,
  Nor one of the things that you dream.

Why do you smile and deny, my lover?
  I will not be denied.
I am book, a book with a cover,
  And nothing at all inside.

Here is the truth, and you must grapple,
  Grapple with what I have said.
I am a dumpling without any apple,
  I am a star that is dead.

THE SICK QUEEN*

I hear my children come. They trample with their feet,
Fetched from their play to kiss my thin-boned hands lying on the sheet,
Fresh as young colts with every field before them,
With gazing apple-faces. Can it be this body bore them?
(This poor body like an outworn glove,
That yet subdues a spirit which no more knows that it can love.)
All day is theirs. I belong to night,
The brown surrounding caverns made of dream. The long failing
    fight,
On and on with pain. Theirs is sweet sleep
And morning breakfast with bright yellow butter. They can laugh
    and weep
Over a tiny thing – a toy, a crumb, a letter.
Tomorrow they will come again and say: *Now* are you better?'
'Better, my lords, today', the Chamberlain replies;
And I shall be too tired and too afraid to cry out that he lies.

---

* I have used the version from *Different Days* rather than from *Collected Poems*.

15

ON AUGUST THE THIRTEENTH
(At The Mount, Marsden, Bucks)

Out of this seemliness, this solid order,
At half-past four to-day,
When down below
Geraniums were bright
In the contented glow,
Whilst Williams planted seedlings all about,
Supremely geometrically right
In your herbaceous border,
You had to go
Who always liked to stay.
Before Louisa sliced the currant roll,
And re-arranged the zinnias in the bowl,
All in a rhythm reachless by modernity,
Correct and slow,
And brought the tea and tray,
At half-past four on Friday you went out:
To the unseemly, seemly,
Dateless, whole
Light of Eternity
You went away.

THE OLD SERVANT
[Original title 'Nurse']

I cannot but believe, though you were dead,
Lying stone-still, and I came in and said
Having been out perhaps in mud and rain:
'O dear, O look, I have torn my skirt again,'
That you would rise with the old simple ease.
And say, 'Yes, child', and come to me. And there
In your white crackling apron, on your knees
With your quick hands, rough with the washing-up
Of every silver spoon and cherished cup,
And bending head, coiled with the happy hair
Your own child should have pulled for you (but no,
Your child who might have been, you did not bear,
Because the endless riches of your care
Were all for us) you would mend and heal my tear –
Mend, touch and heal; and stitching all the while,
Your cottons on the floor, look up and show
The sudden light perpetual of your smile –
Then, with your darning finished, being dead
Go back and lie, like stone, upon your bed.

A BACK VIEW

Now when his hour shall strike
For this old man,
And he arrives in Heaven late
He can
To Peter and the Angel Gabriel,
Having completely known,
Completely tell
What it was like
To lean upon a gate;
And knowing one thing well
He need not fear his fate.

GRAND BALLET

I saw you dance that summer before the war.
One thunderous night it was, at Covent Garden,
When we, who walked, beneath the weighted trees,
Hot metropolitan pavements, might have smelt
Blood in the dust, and heard the traffic's cry
Ceaseless and savage like a prophecy.

As by a sunrise sea I saw you stand,
Your sylphides round you on the timeless strand,
White, pure, delicious poised butterflies,
The early nineteenth century in their eyes,
And Chopin ready for their silver toes.
(O sighs unsatisfied, and one red rose!)

The fountain, of all movement ready to flow
Seemed prisoned in your entranced body. So
You stood, their Prince, most elegantly fair,
Swan-sleeved, black-jacketed, with falling hair
And hands half-raised in ravishment. O there,
Your Grecian arrow fitted to the bow,
You beech-tree in a legendary wood,
You panther in a velvet bolero,
There you for one immortal moment stood –

One moment like a wave before it flows,
Frozen in perfectness. Then one hand rose
And tossed a silver curl, demurely light
(O grace, O rose, O Chopin and all delight),
And the enchantment broke.

                    That thunderous night
We saw Nijinsky dance.
                    Thereafter fell
On the awaiting world the powers of Hell,
Chaos, and irremediable pain;
And utter darkness on your empty brain,
Not even grief to say, No more, no more.

But tell me, when my mortal memories wane
As death draws near, and peace is mine and pardon,
Where will it like an escaped dove repair?
To what Platonic happy heaven – where? –
Untouchable by Fate and free of Time,
That one immortal moment of the mime
We saw Nijinsky dance at Covent Garden?

ODE ON THE WHOLE DUTY OF PARENTS

The spirits of children are remote and wise,
They must go free
Like fishes in the sea
Or starlings in the skies,
Whilst you remain
The shore where casually they come again.
But when there falls the stalking shade of fear,
You must be suddenly near,
You, the unstable, must become a tree
In whose unending heights of flowering green
Hangs every fruit that grows, with silver bells;
Where heart-distracting magic birds are seen
And all the things a fairy-story tells;
Though still you should possess
Roots that go deep in ordinary earth,
And strong consoling bark
To love and to caress.

Last, when at dark
Safe on the pillow lies an up-gazing head
And drinking holy eyes
Are fixed on you,
When, from behind them, questions come to birth
Insistently,
On all the things that you have ever said
Of suns and snakes and parallelograms and flies,
Then for a while you'll need to be no more
That sheltering shore

19

Or legendary tree in safety spread,
No, then you must put on
The robes of Solomon,
Or simply be
Sir Isaac Newton sitting on the bed.

NEIGHBOURS

Old Mrs Thompson down the road is dead.
The maids knew first from what the milkman said,
He heard on Sunday she was very bad,
And as they dust, they are sorry, stirred, and glad.

One day soon I shall die,
As still as Mrs Thompson I shall lie;
And in her house that April day
The maids of the new family will say
That Mrs Jones, who was me, has passed away.
They will know first, because the fish-boy heard;
And as they dust, be sorry, glad, and stirred.

THE PAST
[original title 'Near an Old Prison']

When we would reach the anguish of the dead,
Whose bones alone, irrelevant, are dust,
Out of ourselves we know we must, we must
To some obscure but ever-bleeding thing
Unreconciled, a needed solace bring,
Like a resolving chord, like daylight shed.
Or do we through thick time reach back in vain
To inaccessible pain?

THE LAKE AND THE INSTANT

Have you not seen
The dove-grey waters' undulating sheen
Whereon a bird can rest
Its rounded, slowly, slowly heaving breast,
Whilst all the blue-aired delicate mountains round
Attend, without a sound?
So, freed from fear, man's first primeval crime,
A heart might rest upon the lap of time.

YAMA AND YAMI
[From the Veda]

The first created pair possessed a world
    Where darkness was unknown;
Till Yama died, and left in endless light
    Yami, his twin, alone.

The high Gods tried to comfort her distress,
    But all in vain they tried.
She would not listen to their wisest words;
    She said: 'Today he died.'

Then were the Gods confounded, for her grief
    Troubled their equal sight;
They said: 'In this way she will not forget.
    We must create the Night.'

So they created Night. And after Night
    Came into being Morrow;
And she forgot him. Thus it is they say:
    'The days and nights make men forget their sorrow.'

THE TRUMPET SHALL SOUND
(Messiah 1742)

We who are met to celebrate
Grandly today our God and King and state
   'We shall be changed' – but shall not change too far:
Twice as superb will be, and twice as big
   Each fair, abounding, and immortal wig;
   And every button on our coats, a star.

Where Lords and Commons ever equal are
Each regal coach will grow a wingèd car,
Whose laurelled lackeys in triumphant light
Sing their symmetrical delight;
And link-boys with the flaming cherubim
Dance in their buckled shoes and shout the morning hymn;
Where coachmen crowned with ashphodel and moly
Echo the cries of Holy, Holy, Holy;
And disembodied horses fly
With golden trumpeters about the sky.

O we shall change, but with no pangs of birth,
To glorious heaven from this glorious earth.

THE SINGLE WOMAN

Now quenched each midnight window is. Now unimpeded
   Darkness descends on roof and tree and slope;
And in my heart the houses that you have not needed
   Put out their lights of comfort and of hope.

A PEASANT WOMAN

I saw you sit waiting with your sewing on your knees,
Till a man should claim the comfort of your body
And your industry and presence for his own.

I saw you sit waiting with your sewing on your knees,
Till the child growing hidden in your body
Should become a living creature in the light.

I saw you sit waiting with your sewing on your knees,
Till your child who had ventured to the city
Should return to the shelter of his home.

I saw you sit waiting with your sewing on your knees
– Your unreturning son was in the city –
Till Death should come along the cobbled street.

I saw you sit waiting with your sewing on your knees.

CONSTANT

When you awake at dawn in Paradise,
Who sheltered all men like an apple-tree,
What, after many years and pain unknown,
In dew-gray fields beneath celestial skies,
What would your first desired fulfilment be?

That he who loved you and who died alone,
Should on your warm lap lie,
To faint and die;
The lovely hair fallen back upon your knee;
The eyes that shut alone closed by your kiss
And washed by your own tears. It would be this.

MOTHER TO CHILD ASLEEP

These tiny, fringed eyes
Must look on all that dies;
In some strange dawn with bleeding tears perceive
This house they now believe
Coeval with its dome
Of arching sky, this home
Which an unending tabernacle seems,
Dissolve like dreams –
This tree-tall clock, that sempiternal door,
The table white for dinner, all no more.

Ah, though I might, no magic must be willed
On your vexed waters, vexed when mine are stilled.
On that strange morning you must sail alone,
My utterly-sleeping own.

THE END

This effigy that was a man reposes;
All questions cease.
Yet fire, and snakes, and roses,
Jungles of pain, and sudden pools of peace
Were in this packed tumultuous heart, that here
Unbeating lies beneath the purple of the bier.

And so much more, much more, much more,
So strange a medley and so infinite a store
No thought can compass and no music say
Upon his burial day.

FAIRY-TALE IDYLL FOR TWO VOICES

O sing or tell a story. What shall I tell?
There was a Princess woke at early dawn,
A Princess in a castle, in the north,
And saw the forests rising tree on tree
Out of her little window, and ran forth
To look for berries in the autumn woods.
O sing of what she found in the woods as well.

She must slip away before the kitchen stirs,
With hooded golden hair, down garden walks,
Past home-faced apples, over the open ground
Where feed her father's herd of cream-white cows,
With swinging tails and delicate, peaceful feet
Among the mountain crocuses, with bells
Like hope and dew, and come to the edge of the woods.
Brave she must be, for in the woods are bears;
The noise of waters fills them like a breath
And footsteps make no sound. At home they tell
The king of the bears is an enchanted Prince
Who waits release. But who shall break the spell?

The forests rise around her tree on tree,
To cloud-high crags; they rise round secret lawns
Where red ash-berries for no human hand
Drop. And she listens. If she listens long
She hears clear voices, voices of surprise,
Wonder and argument and prophecies,
Hid in the streams. For whom to understand?
She only feels a spirit, that is hers,
Tells her to climb, to climb and fear no ills,
To fear no presence in the unpeopled woods,
Or hidden in the caverns of the hills.
.She can but tell how swiftly she must start
Up, up the paths where only hunters go,
Running with silver shoes that make no mark,
Quick with a purpose that she cannot know
And singing unawares.

Wet bilberries and scarlet cranberries
Four-leaved Herb Paris with his sorcerer's heart,
Whose home is in the stillness under trees,
And black strange cherries, strange with double stones –
O all of these,
Tell how she plucked them with her weaving hands
To make a wreath of berries bright and dark,
And some that shone like blood in the early sun,
To make a wreath, a wreath for whom begun?
To make a garland for the king of the bears.
And then, O tell
How all at once her singing voice was dumb
And her heart fell.

Fierce-eyed and hairy round a jutting rock
Dark, dark and softly-footing he was there,
The king of the woods, the black enchanted bear,
Unpassably, unconquerably come.
But quickly, now tell this:
How she was brave, how she was not afraid,
She flung the wreath of berries round his neck,
The ripple of her amber-yellow hair
Sweeping his claws and pouring from her hood,
Her young thin arms, her oval cheek in fur,
And made him captive, captive with a kiss.

And suddenly, suddenly, there
Slant-eyed and smiling the leaf-strewn light,
Silent as moss, and all the streams his speech,
A Prince was standing in the bilberry wood,
Proud and delivered in the world of men.
Right through the trees the sun ascending burned
In wealth of swaying gold his glorious way,
And wrapped in light and shadow each to each
No spoken word need say,
For in the arisen morning there he stands,
Free from his cavern's airless echoing space,
Safe from the dark compulsion of his form.

Sing how he looked at her with eyes returned
From exile to the harbour of her face,
To certainty from storm;
And touched her shoulders with his stranger's hands,
With hands grown more familiar in an hour
Than all her home and years of yesterday,
The unilluminated years before.
O sing and tell of this, and tell no more,
But how, as on the first created day
All things were new,
And through the tall-stemmed forest, far below,
Before they turned in harmony to go,
The clustered berries round their shoulders wound.
Before they reached the fruitful open ground
They heard the bells of feeding flocks, the sound
Like hope and dew.

TRAVELLING HOME

The train. A hot July. On either hand
Our sober, fruitful, unemphatic land,
This Cambridge country plain beneath the sky
Where I was born, and grew, and hope to die.

Look! where the willows hide a rushy pool,
And the old horse goes squelching down to cool,
One angler's rod against their silvery green,
Still seen today as once by Bewick seen.

A cottage there, thatched badly, like its earth,
Where crimson ramblers make a shortlived mirth;
Here, only flies the flick-tail cows disturb
Among the shaven meads and willow-herb.

There, rounded hay-ricks solemn in the yard,
Barns gravely, puritanically tarred,
Next heavy elms that guard the ripening grain
And fields, and elms, and corn, and fields again.

Over the soft savannahs of the corn,
Like ships the hot white butterflies are borne,
While clouds pass slowly on the flower-blue dome
Like spirits in a vast and peaceful home.

Over the Dyke I watch their shadows flow
As the Icenian watched them long ago;
So let me in this Cambridge calm July
Fruitfully live and undistinguished die.

WAKING IN THE ATTIC BEDROOM

More innocently born and calmer seems
In its soft summer haze
This Sunday morning than all other days.
No early footsteps walk into my dreams,
A peace is everywhere
As if the whole created world believed in prayer,
Over the solitary fields of wheat,
And down the village street,
And on my folded clothes across the chair.

THE CORNER OF THE FIELD

Here the young lover, on his elbow raised,
Looked at his happy girl with grass surrounded,
And flicked the spotted beetle from her wrist:
She, with her head thrown back, at heaven gazed,
At Suffolk clouds, serene and slow and mounded;
Then calmly smiled at him before they kissed.

THE VISIT

There is a bed-time sadness in this place
That seemed ahead so promising and sweet,
Almost like music calling us from home;

But now the staircase does not need our feet,
The drawer is ignorant of my brush and comb
The mirror quite indifferent to your face.

CHILDHOOD

I used to think that grown-up people chose
To have stiff backs and wrinkles round their nose,
And veins like small fat snakes on either hand,
On purpose to be grand.
Till through the bannisters I watched one day
My great-aunt Etty's friend who was going away,
And how her onyx beads had come unstrung.
I saw her grope to find them as they rolled;
And then I knew that she was helplessly old,
As I was helplessly young.

TO A YOUNG CAT IN THE ORCHARD

Elegant creature with black shoulders bent,
Stalking the bird in song,
To what intent?
Tell what a wild source brims those empty eyes,
What well of shameless light,
Beyond the bounds of Hell or Paradise
Or wrong
Or right.

IN THE BACKS

Too many of the dead, some I knew well,
Have smelt this unforgotten river smell,
Liquid and old and dank;
And on the tree-dark, lacquered, slowly passing stream
Have seen the boats come softly as in dream
Past the green bank.
So Camus, reverend sire, came footing slow
Three hundred years ago,
And Milton paced the avenue of trees
In miracle of sun and shade as now,
The fresh-attempted glorious cadences
Behind his youthful brow.

Milton and Chaucer, Herbert, Herrick, Gray,
Rupert, and you forgotten others, say –
Are there slow rivers and bridges where you have gone away?
What has your spirit found? What wider lot?
Some days in spring do you come back at will,
And tread with weightless feet the ancient ground?
O say, if not,
Why is this air so sacred and so still?

FAMILY LIKENESS

That eager, honouring look
Through microscope or at a picture-book,
That quick, responsive, curious delight –
For half a century I have seen it now
Under the shaggy or the baby brow,
And always blessed the sight.

AFTER THE EXAMINATION

When someone's happy in a house there shows
A chink of honey-coloured light beneath the bedroom door,
Where once a thunder-purple gloom oozed out across the floor;
And even the stairs smell like an early rose.

THE GRANDSON DRESSES UP

James painted black moustaches round his nose,
And in the glass a sneering Satan smiled.
I thought once more how harrowingly glows
Beneath the cork the innocence of a child.

GONE DOWN

No longer will his name be found
Beside the College stair;
White-lettered on the old black ground
Another name is there.
In the calm court new footsteps sound,
In courts too calm to care.

BEDROOM DAWN

Is this obscurity not quite unbroken,
As though the heart of night had bled away,
This quietness before a bird has spoken
Really the day?

And is this depth of darkness redefined,
The safe diurnal washing-stand and soap,
This first small stir of the awakened mind,
Possibly hope?

THE COAST: NORFOLK

As on the highway's quiet edge
He mows the grass beside the hedge,
The old man has for company
The distant, grey, salt-smelling sea,
A poppied field, a cow and calf,
The finches on the telegraph.

Across his faded back a hone,
He slowly, slowly scythes alone
In silence of the wind-soft air,
With ladies' bedstraw everywhere,
With whitened corn and tarry poles,
And far-off gulls like risen souls.

BICKER'S COTTAGE

Companionable ticking of the clock;
Collapsing of the coal;
The chair-legs warm;
Tobacco in a bowl;
The door sealed up;
The sooted kettle's hiss;
The firelit loaf; the cocoa-tin; the cup;
Outside, the unplumbed night and pattering storm.

At such an hour as this
A ghost might knock,
Lacking unearthly comfort in its soul.

SUMMER BEACH

For how long known this boundless wash of light,
    This smell of purity, this gleaming waste,
This wind? This brown, strewn wrack how old a sight,
    These pebbles round to touch and salt to taste.

See, the slow marbled heave, the liquid arch,
    Before the waves' procession to the land
Flowers in foam; the ripples' onward march,
    Their last caresses on the pure hard sand.

For how long known these bleaching corks, new-made
    Smooth and enchanted from the lapping sea?
Since first I laboured with a wooden spade
    Against this background of Eternity.

MORNING PRAYER

My hands, O Lord, receive the crystal day,
Let me preserve it whole for evermore,
And grey-broomed evening find to sweep away
No fragments on the floor.

BEHIND THE GREEK RESTAURANT

The Cypriot woman, as she closed her dress,
Smiled at the baby on her broad-lapped knee,
Beautiful in a calm voluptuousness
Like a slow sea.

THE OLD WOMAN IN SPRING

I envy your contorted bole,
You ancient tree. By every soul
Your youthfulness of heart is seen,
Because you fountain into green.

Unaltered as in winter now
My twisted hands and wrinkled brow;
Yet my heart, too, though none believes,
Is happy with a thousand leaves.

PARTING IN PEACETIME

When we had reached the gate I raised my eyes
And, kissing you good night, I laughed and said
I feared the stars might strike you from the skies,
Like crystal stones on your too happy head.

PARTING IN WARTIME

How long ago Hector took off his plume,
Not wanting that his little son should cry,
Then kissed his sad Andromache goodbye –
And now we three in Euston waiting-room.

FROM A LETTER TO AMERICA ON A VISIT TO SUSSEX: SPRING 1942

How simply violent things
Happen, is strange.
How strange it was to see
In the soft Cambridge sky our Squadron's wings,
And hear the huge hum in the familiar grey.
And it was odd today
On Ashdown Forest that will never change,
To find a gunner in the gorse, flung down,
Well-camouflaged, and bored and lion brown.
A little further by those twisted trees
(As if it rose on humped preposterous seas
Out of a Book of Hours) up a bank
Like a large dragon, purposeful though drunk,
Heavily lolloped, swayed and sunk,
A tank.
All this because manoeuvres had begun.
But now, but soon,
At home on any usual afternoon,
High overhead
May come Erinyes winging.
Or here the boy may lie beside his gun,
His mud-brown tunic gently staining red,
While larks get on with their old job of singing.

THE FACE IN THE OPPOSITE CORNER

– Why frown? Why stare?
– My heart's a cell, rock-walled,
  Defaced and scrawled,
  And there
  The secret blood runs down.
  That's why I frown.

CASUALTIES

This once protected flesh the War-god uses
Like any gadget of a great machine;
This flesh once pitied where a gnat had been,
And kissed with passion on invisible bruises.

AUTUMN BLITZ

Unshaken world! Another day of light
After the human chaos of the night;
Although a heart in mendless horror grieves,
What calmly yellow, gently falling leaves!

SOLDIERS ON THE PLATFORM

Look how these young, bare, bullock faces know,
With a simplicity like drawing breath,
That out of happiness we fall on woe
And in the midst of life we are in death.

See how in staring sameness each one stands,
His laden shoulders, and his scoured hands;
But each behind his wall of flesh and bone
Thinks with this secret he is armed alone.

A FRIEND

On days when you have been
Unhappy, lonely, ill,
Your spirit I have seen
Receiving, listening still.

On mornings when my kind
Seem all a conquered race,
Then I recall to mind
I have seen your risen face.

THE TRUE EVIL

When he was questioned at the time of the trial –
This is a truth I once refused to know –
Peter outside in the yard denied his Master,
And heard, immediately, the cock crow.

But now I have known a more complete disaster,
An empty horror Peter never knew,
When I was questioned, after my denial
No cock crew.

FOR J.R. – ON ELISABETH SINGING

You who, frustrated, died so long ago
In night and pain, but left a child to grow;
Passionate spirit, in the shades rejoice;
All that you suffered and knew is in her voice.

FIGURES ON THE PLATFORM

Travelling at night no man has any home
Beyond the station's melancholy dome.
The giant tired engine starts again
For homeless fields anonymous in rain,
Now it has gone. But that was not our train.
Even the kit-bag and the trundled can
Are cared-for and considered more than man
Who has been travelling since his life began.

COUNTRY IDYLL

Deep in the stable tied with rope,
The cow has neither dignity nor hope.

With ugly, puzzled, hot despair
She needs the calf that is not there,
And mourns and mourns him to unheeding air.

But if the sleeping farmer hears,
He pulls the blanket higher round his ears.

BENEFACTORS

Still the medieval hunger to atone
Troubles the secret heart of men today,
And still they know no penitence prolonged,
No costly, ornate edifice of stone
Can ever wash the finished past away,
Nor thank the dead they intimately wronged.

THE SCHOLAR

You often went to breathe a timeless air
And walk with those you loved, perhaps the most
You spoke to Plato. You were native there.
Like one who made blind Homer sing to him,
You visited the caves where sirens swim
Their deep-indented coast.
                  With us you seemed
A quiet happy sailor come of late
From those strange seas you best could navigate,
Knowing a world that others only dreamed.
Almost we looked for spray upon your hair,
Who met you, silent-footed on the stair,
Like an Elysian ghost.
                So on that day
You left us on a deep withdrawing tide,
We dared not beg you, with one sigh, to stay
Or turn from your discoveries aside.

THE CONSCRIPT

In summer months when he was four
   And used a wooden spade,
Bill Turner floated from this shore
   The boats his father made.

Now he, a soldier, sails from home
   On wild December ways,
Remembering the gentle foam
   And those protected days.

A WARTIME SKETCH

Drink the unflowing waters with green hair
You Cambridge willows, calm and unaware;
Soon he will vanish like a summer's midge,
That calm-struck soldier leaning on the bridge,
And things be always as they always were.

THE HERD

How calmly cows move to the milking sheds,
How slowly, hieratically along,
How humbly with their moon-surmounted heads,
Though fly-pursued and stained, they pass me by
As gravely as the clouds across the sky,
They being, like the stars 'preserved from wrong'.

THE OLD WOMAN AT THE FLOWER SHOW

Come inside the swinging gate
And pay your pennies for the Fête,
Where once I strolled with all the rest
In my sash and Sunday best.

Dust and ash the eyes I sought,
Where I strolled and strayed and sat,
And the rose my mother bought
To stick inside my shady hat,
His blue eyes and my bright sash,
        Dust and ash.

THE QUARREL

How simple is my burden every day
  Now you have died, till I am also dead,
The words 'Forgive me', that I could not say,
    The words 'I am sorry', that you might have said.

TWO YEARS OLD

A child that prospers, carries everywhere
A little dome of pleasant secret air,
We, who receive his unconcerned embrace
    Perceive it, sacred, round the soft-nosed face.

AFTER THE PARTY

Banish the scent of sherry and cigars
    Throw back the shutters, quench the cultured light,
Let in the air. O fresher than the stars
    The rank, primeval innocent smell of night.

FOR NIJINSKY'S TOMB

Nijinsky's ashes here in peace repose
No more the Faun, the Harlequin, the Rose.

We saw him framed in light before the crowds,
Hushed like a tree that waits the touch of dawn,
A panther ready, or an arrow drawn.
Then music came, the sure, awakening bars,
He leapt beyond the bounds of joy and grief:
His heart conferred in those transfigured hours,
Strength like the sun, precision like the stars;
The sea was his; the buoyancy of clouds,
The sap that flows in every fluted leaf,
The blossoming, in light, of fields and flowers.
Yet later, smiling in applauded grace,
The Faun, the Rose was never wholly ours,
We saw remoteness in the tilted face,
He heard alone, beyond our human ears,
Beyond applause, the Music of the Spheres.

Nijinsky's ashes here in peace are laid
Their perfect tribute to Perfection paid.

TWO EPITAPHS:

For Charlotte Brontë in Haworth Church Yard

The children of my fiery heart and brain
Endure, created, like the wind and rain
            Imperishably wild.
But near this stone, and in this iron air,
I died, because my body could not bear
            A mortal child.

On a Pet

Florence has lost her joy, her marmoset.
No more those bright world-penetrating eyes
Peer from the sacred cavern of her muff,
Two jewels closely set.
Un-nibbled now the sugared cherry lies,
November sleet whips through the northern skies,
The tiny tropic heart has throbbed enough.

JOURNEYS END IN LOVERS' MEETING

I. At a Dinner Party

– Jean, let me introduce Sir Robert Frazer,
   But once in Wiltshire years ago you met,
   Don't you remember?
                      – Yes, I can't forget...
   Our Hostess acts the imbecile, it pays her.
   – You always were so horrid about people.
   – And you were always bringing out their best.
   – Bob, do behave like any other guest...
     Do you remember Wagdon Prior steeple
     And how it rises out of Salisbury plain?
   – I dislike steeples seen at any angle,
   – How strange that we should only meet to wrangle.
   – Frankly, I hope we never shall again.
   – But do say something in this awful lull,
     You always had the gift of being dull.

II. *In a Cambridge Garden*

– Bill, take a cushion on the ground, that's better!
  Just how you used to lie ten years ago.
– Tell me one thing I have a right to know,
  Why did you never answer my last letter?
– I used to wish when I was seventeen
  (You can't chew grass *and* make a noble face)
  That I could find that fairy-story place
  Where there is everything that might have been.
  That treasured kitten grown Eternal Cat,
  The plays we meant to act in, you and I,
  Even the tears there was never time to cry,
  Do you think Heaven was really always that,
  Not harps and halos?
                                  – Clare, I know it well
  And go there often, but its name is Hell.

Epitaph for a Reviewer

Whoso maintains that I am humbled now
  (Who wait the Awful Day) is still a liar;
I hope to meet my Maker brow to brow
  And find my own the higher.

THE PAST

Astonishment is on me unaware
At the absolute sameness of spring on altering hair,
At spring's identical embroidered riches,
At the same stitchwort flowering in hot ditches,
At cowslips, clustered, smelling humbly sweet,
Still with their round pale stalks which are good to eat,
Though now the child who closely knew these things
Is lost along a corridor of springs.

TWO OLD MEN OUTSIDE AN INN

Somewhat their shoulders have begun to bow
As if in deference to earth, who now
May any day invite them to be done
Quite quietly with bench and beer and sun.

AUCTION AT THE COTTAGE

This spade and barrow by the fence
Were Bicker's tools for forty springs,
And use, how well, the eloquence
Of often-handled voiceless things.

THE RUIN

Here a home has split in half,
Nettles make its epitaph.
On their venomed surface lies
No dew from gentle skies;
They with acrid sombre smell
(Shards and rubble know it well)
Come to occupy the scene
Where our angry lives have been.

IN THE EGYPTIAN ROOM

This is your mummy-case, the experts say,
You who were Priest of the Theban Temple of Amen Ra
And though around its regal sides are shown
Scenes that should end a journey each must start alone,
Two thousand years after your final breath
Your golden face is still absorbed discovering death.
In the Infirmary across the way
An unknown lorry-driver died to-day.
Gone are the accidents of time and place,
Initiate, stern, hieratic, lies a brother face.

ON CHILDREN

How dull our days, how lacking in surprise
Without these small epitomes of sin,
These flowers with their store of life within
And grave, appalling freshness in their eyes.

GROWN UP

We pity children playing when we see
Their concrete joys have such fragility.
But can we even show a trampled toy
To justify our constant lack of joy?

THE GHOST: A BALLAD

Still-born brother, never known,
  They told me as a boy
You had gone to far-off lands
  And there grew up in joy.

But when I played in solitude
  I wished I had a twin,
I wished that you could open doors
  And come out and in.

And now I sit an ageing man
  And stare into the grate,
Still my mind is set on you
  And still I wait.

Can I by a wordless spell
  Can I by a prayer
Summon you on All Souls' Night
  To overlean my chair?

Have you left those far-off lands
  For a little space?
Did you with your unborn hands
  Just touch my face?

CHRISTMAS LULLABY

There was neither grass nor corn
In the fields when Christ was born:
No my dearest treasure no,
All the fields were white with snow,
All the fields were smooth and white
And shepherds watched their flocks by night.

48

In the fields where nothing stirred
Listen what the shepherds heard:
'Bare bare fields rejoice',
Hear the angel's silver voice:
'You have neither grass nor corn
You are rich for Christ is born'.

DUSK

This is the owl moment I have always known,
Not yet completely dark,
When small birds twit him in the park,
In terror though they tease.
Out he comes among the trees,
He comes on oiled wings, alone,
And mice and tucked-up children hear
His long to-whoo as old as fear.

POET DEFEATED

Moon in your perfect phase,
You fruit of night,
Too ancient for a fashionable phrase,
For faded adjectives too undefiled,
Uncapturable moon you are with child
And great with light.

SLEEPLESSNESS

O what wide shore,
What vision of a plain
By the last bird deserted, and last light,
Will lead me from this labyrinth of pain,
Absolve me from my bone-surrounded brain,
In amplitude of night
To ache no more.

UNKNOWN

Near midnight
All winds cease
And give to darkness peace.
Then nothing wakes,
Then darkness takes
Silence for a lover:
What, beyond sight,
Throngs the ceiling, when
Darkness sleeps and men?

Nobody can discover.

UNWELCOME MORNING

Receiving night,
Anonymous and whole,
This prying grey
Must never grow and change your seamless soul
To complicated day.
Then every bird will start to do you wrong
And praise the light
In clear particular song:
But you are mine to keep.
O I will turn and burrow back to sleep
And thrust this multiplicity away.

THE AVENUE

Who has not seen their lover
Walking at ease,
Walking like any other
A pavement under trees,
Not singular, apart,
But footed, featured, dressed,
Approaching like the rest
In the same dapple of the summer caught;
Who has not suddenly thought
With swift surprise:
There walks in cool disguise,
There comes, my heart?

THE LIVING GIRL
TO THE DEAD ONE

You never will come
   You never can hear,
O what did you do
   To your only dear?

This fog of death
   I can't *see* through,
O were you false to him
   Were you true?

Were you a Cressid
   Born to be,
As innocent leaves
   Must cover a tree?

Your puzzled eyes
   Your ivory brow
Your April hair
   Are gone away now,

And all those gifts
   That spring-time gave
Before you took them
   Into the grave.

O were they for one
   Or were they for two?
And were you false to your love
   Or true?

THE YOUNG MAN TO HIS GIRL

The new geography behind your eyes
May I not read, and come, and colonise?
Why should we stand like continents apart?
Let me embark for your insistent shore
And the Virginia of your pathless heart
              Explore.

A YOUNG LOVE AFFAIR

Caught in this whirl of love and hate,
   How could I find your inward heart?
For now I see, and see too late,
Caught in this whirl of love and hate,
Our choreographer was fate
   By whose design we move apart.
Caught in this whirl of love and hate,
   How could I find your inward heart?

HE SAYS GOODBYE IN NOVEMBER

You say you know that nature never grieves:
I also see the acquiescent leaves
Fall down and rot
As down the derelict statue runs the rain;
But you believe that spring will come again
And I do not.

A SEPARATION ON THE SHORE

He That soft sea-weed is your heart
      Did you know?
      And this bleaching bone
      My own.

She I read a ballad long ago
       About two lovers kept apart:
       Two roses, white and red,
       Joined their graves
                        when they were dead:
       Their own hearts, the ballad said.

He Why cry? There is no need.
      O have pity, let me go.
      Nothing, nothing can unite
      A sensual weed,
      A bone bleached white.

SEASIDE MORNING

How gaily flock and fleet behave
   As if the one the other were;
Boats, shining, fly across the wave,
   Gulls float across the shining air.

LINCOLNSHIRE LANDSCAPE

Wind from the Steppes unopposed, unaware
All will not yield to you, sweep the corn's hair,
Ruffle the bullocks, slant low the buttercups,
Chuck up the magpies in the huge air:
Farms that are islanded, safe in their sycamores,
Tiled with placidity, they will not care.

THE GRANITE FIREPLACE

I sit beside the logs alone
And search the surface of the stone:
Soon to my idling eyes appear
The soft suggestions of a deer,
A dolphin leaping from the seas
And blossomed paradisal trees;
But horrid on the harmless rock
Hitler's face and falling lock.

AUGUST AT HOME

How rich the elms, and large, and summer-sad,
    My childhood trees;
I thought of them as people, when I had
    No words for them like these.
I drink their presence, and I go my ways,
    They bring no altered mood;
These heavy trees are part of all my days,
    Like sleep they are, and food.

ON A CALM SHORE

You lulling sea
Like Circe innocent
(Who of necessity
Was the enchantress that she had to be)
Soft sea, do you believe
You can, like her, so perfectly deceive,
With gentle foam?
Though brown Ulysses smiled
In calm content,
Her face his home,
The very pebbles that your skill has ground,
Your simple sound,
Are not by any interlude beguiled;
They understand
Deep in their quiet core
Your absolute might,
They know in winter that tyrannic sound,
Your thunder up the shore,
On them have lain all night
The heavy drowned.

ESPLANADE MOOD

How many faces raddled and afraid
How many beings opulently petty
With corns and corgies hobble this parade:
Eternity unwatched beyond the jetty.

AT THE CIRCUS

His secret grievous dreadful eyes
   Belie the grin and painted frown,
Still through his acts antiquely rise
   The terrors of a Roman clown.

HIGH TIDE

Waves, as you ride to flood the stagnant dyke
   And heal the sands with your recurrent art,
Immaculate and proud and business-like,
   Sweep and restore my heart.

AN IMPRESSION IN THE TUILERIES GARDENS

Zeus is descending through the summer leaves
The avenue's majestic human height,
And Danae-like the simple ground receives
The passion of the light;
Glad through the swaying scattered coins of sun
The children and the shaven poodles run.

Far down the prospect of umbrageous trees
Receding statues rise in florid grace,
An Amphitrite or a Hercules
Infallibly in place,
As though an earthly garden might rehearse
The width and order of a universe.

The prams and poodles and the running boys,
The resting tramps, receive the classic hour,
Whilst couples court on chairs as green as toys,
And striped umbrellas flower,
And old-accustomed humble people sit,
Chequered with joy, and gently benefit.

ITALIAN SIESTA

Come from the glare to find
Your shuttered room most welcomingly blind
And white dimmed pillows on a waiting bed
That need your instant head.
This is no hour for sight,
Outside the colours are consumed by light;
The knitting women in the narrow street
Nod in the heat;
Flung down on his bleached nets
The fisherman forgets
Even the morning's catch he went to make
Where white rocks glisten under the hot lake.
Only the dry cicadas are awake
And scraping unremittingly repeat
A sound which is the very soul of heat.
There is no thought your dazzled mind can keep.
Come here and sleep.

ON MAOU: A CAT AGED SIX MONTHS

Strange sickness fell upon this perfect creature
Who walked at equal ease with man and nature;
Now wrapped in fever like a sultry cloud,
He helpless lay, who once was sleek and proud,
Till to his eyes, unasking yet afraid,
The old reply of endless night was made.

EPITAPH FOR EVERYMAN

My heart was more disgraceful, more alone,
And more courageous than the world has known.

O passer-by, my heart was like your own.

MISSING

With what an absolute reproach
      Lost things lie,
Dead soldiers or unposted letters
      Watched by the sky.

'You dropped us,' say our fallen letters
      Innocently clear.
The corpses: 'Your indifference
      Laid us here.'

WAITING IN HOSPITAL

These fragments I have shored against my ruin

This dominant machine,
These forms, these files,
This self-assured routine,
Cylindered oxygen for gasping breath,
White antiseptic tiles,
Clattering heels and smiles,
Each fragment of this regulated hour
Innocent man has shored against the power
Of ruinous death.

NIJINSKY

The Muse Terpsichore
Long, long abandoned me,
And left an empty shell
Confused by dreams from hell.

Yet from lucid skies
She'll call me when she will,
And weeping I shall rise
And be her servant still.

THE GUITARIST TUNES UP

With what attentive courtesy he bent

Over his instrument;
Not as a lordly conqueror who could

Command both wire and wood,
But as a man with a loved woman might,

Inquiring with delight
What slight essential things she had to say
Before they started, he and she, to play.

A CARNIVAL DREAM

I saw a motley pirouetting crowd, and asked:
Why are they masked?

But I already knew how each must go,
Each in his dark concealing domino,
Brother concealed from brother, friend from friend,
To the very end.

I saw an infant, swung and swayed to rest,
Suck in a little mask his mother's breast,
And whirling lovers in a long embrace
Who never could perceive each other's hidden face.

ON A YOUNG FACE AT THE OPERA

Soon they must fade those cheek-bones petal-rounded
And that unwritten forehead, hyacinth-hair surrounded,
Soon says the ruthless ever-ticking year,
And *soon* the silver music of *Der Rosenkavalier*.

EXEUNT OMNES

Your gracefully exhausted servants stand
Receiving thanks with thanks and hand in hand.

I never see the players take their call
With such an ancient and accomplished art
Without the whole allegiance of my heart,
For now both high and low at curtain-fall
Each playing perfectly his equal part
Convey the evanescence of us all.

From

POEMS FROM THE RUSSIAN

Chosen and translated by Frances Cornford and
Esther Polianowsky Salaman

London, Faber and Faber, 1943

IVAN KRYLOV (1768-1844)

THE WOLF IN THE KENNELS

A wolf one night, marauding after sheep,
Found himself in the kennels with the hounds.
At once the whole yard, roused from sleep,
Was filled with furious sounds.
Scenting the old grey bully near,
The dogs, all frantic for the fray-
Leap at the bars and bay;
'A thief' the huntsmen yell:
'A thief's broke in! Here, fellows, here!'
The gates are locked; the yard is turned to hell.
The men come running fast;
One grabs a club, another brings a gun;
Lights, lights! they clamour as they run,
And lights are brought at last.

Tail squeezed into a corner, there he sits,
Bristling, with chattering teeth and sharpened wits.
His eyes would have devoured them all with ease,
But well he knows, no sheep are these,
And for those sheep he has been wont to slay
The hour has struck at last when he must pay.
The cunning creature starts to feel his way
Into a parley, and begins like this:
'Good friends, why all this uproar? What's amiss?
I'm your old kinsman. Here is some mistake.
I come to talk of peace and not to wrangle –
Let's look at things from a more modern angle.
Let us forget the past and break
Fresh ground – set up together a New Order.
Not only will I undertake
Never to touch a sheep within your border,
But from henceforth I'll make it my delight
Myself in their defence to fight.
I swear by a wolf's honour uncorrupted:
'Your coat is grey, but I'm grey-headed too,
And I know you
And all your wiles of old, and just what's in 'em;

65

And therefore, neighbour, 'tis my use
To have no truck with wolves except to skin 'em.'
With that he let the whole pack loose.

ALEXANDER PUSHKIN (1768-1844)

THE POET

When the poet by Apollo
For his service is not claimed,
In a life inane and hollow
He is sunken, he is maimed.
Then his soul, as cold as clay,
Sleeps unvisited by Song:
He frequents the worldly throng,
Insignificant as they.
But let once Apollo's word
Fall upon his listening ear,
His awakened soul is stirred.
Like an eagle soaring clear.
Wild and sad, he turns away
From the pleasures of the town,
Scorning man and man's renown
And the idols of a day.
Full of voices, in the trees
Of confusion forth he goes,
Lonely, to the forest trees
And the shores of barren seas.

THE CRUCIFIX

When the last great and solemn act was played
And God in torment on the cross was laid
Then at the foot of the life-giving rood
Mary the sinner and Mary the Virgin stood,
Two women side by side,
Drowned in their grief's immeasurable tide.

But here beneath the cross we contemplate,
As though on duty at the Governor's gate,
Instead of those two holy women, lo,
Two sentries grim, with musket and shako.
Now tell me, Why? This crucifix, maybe,
You guard in state as Government property?
Or thieves, or mice, you fancy, might lay siege?
Or to the King of Kings you'd add prestige?
Or do you hope by patronage to save
The Lord who is crowned with thorns, the Lord who gave
In willingness His mortal flesh to bear
The Roman torturer's lash, the nails, the spear?
Or else you fear the mob may bring disgrace
On Him who dying saved all Adam's race?
Or, lest his presence irk the modish crowd,
The common man, perhaps, is Not Allowed?

EXEGI MONUMENTUM

I raised a monument not built with hands.
	A nation's path will lead to it. There grows
No grass upon the way. More proud it stands
	Than ever Alexandrian column rose.

Not all of me shall die, for in my song
	There lives a soul outlasting mortal things;
My fame will walk upon the earth as long
	As underneath the moon one poet sings.

Through Russia's length and breadth from age to age
        In her hundred tongues I shall be named
By Tartars, Finns, the Slav's proud lineage,
        And Kalmuk riders of the Steppe untamed.

Long will my people love me, great and small,
        Because in man for men I woke goodwill;
I called for mercy on the fallen soul,
        And in this despot age praised freedom still.

God's will obey, my Muse, and walk His ways,
        Demand no laurels, from no insult fly,
Be heedless both of calumny and praise,
        And to the cavilling fool make no reply.

MIHAIL LERMONTOV (1814-41)

THE TESTAMENT

How much I wanted them to go
And let me be alone with you!
They say I can't last long: I know,
Brother, that what they say is true.

You'll soon be getting leave, no doubt.
Look here – but no; when I pass out
I think there's no one over there
Who'll worry much for that, or care.

So let it be; but if they do
Ask after me – no matter who –
Tell them what happened: you can say
I stopped a bullet yesterday.

Tell them I fought for home and Tsar,
And say what fools the doctors are,
And how to the old country I
Said you must say for me good-bye.

I don't suppose Mother and Dad
Are still alive; but if they were,
What should you say? I wouldn't care,
I must confess, to make them sad.

So, if they're living, he or she,
Just say they mustn't fret for me:
Tell them the regiment's been fighting,
And I was always bad at writing.

There was a girl who lived near-by;
Perhaps she has forgot my name;
So long ago we said good-bye,
She may not ask; but all the same.

Tell her what's happened, plain and bare;
That empty heart you need not spare;
Just let her cry and have her say;
Tears cost her nothing, anyway.

MY COUNTRY

I love my country with a singular love
That reason cannot move:
'Tis not her glory
Bought with our Russian blood, nor her proud story
Of strength impregnable, nor heritage
Of legends handed down from age to age.
That stirs my dreams. But I must testify:
These things I love, and cannot tell you why.

Rivers in flood like seas,
Deep in her woods the swaying of the trees,
In the cold fields her silence – I love these.

Those endless days
Jolting my cart along her dusty ways,
Till, sighing for a place to spend the night,
And peering through the darkness left and right,
Far off one sees
The trembling lights of her sad villages.

I love the wispy smoke
From the singed stubble-fields on soft winds borne;
The covered wagons of the wandering folk
In the wide steppes asleep when day is done;
And on the hill among the yellow corn
The two white birches shining in the sun.

With comfort few can share,
I love to see a barn filled full of hay,
Or the poor huts straw-covered by the way,
With rough-carved shutters round their windows bare –
And many a feast-day evening I am found,
Eager to watch upon the dewy ground,
Till dawn is near,
The tramp and whistle of the dance, and hear
The drunken babble round.

NIKOLAY NEKRASOV (1821-77)

A HYMN

Lord, give them freedom who are weak
And sanctify the people's ways,
Grant them the justice which they seek,
And bless their labouring days.

May freedom, but a seed at first,
Untrammelled rise to flower and spread.
For knowledge let the people thirst,
And light the path ahead.

Lord, set your chosen followers free,
Release them from their ancient bands,
Entrust the flag of liberty
At last, to Russian hands.

FEDOR TYUTCHEW (1803-73)

THE BEGGAR

My God, send down Thy consolation
To him who on the pavement's heat,
Past the green garden, like a beggar,
    Drags heavy feet;

To him who sees beyond the paling
Smooth lawns where cool the shadows lie,
Green hollows that he may not enter,
    But passes by.

No, not for him the trees in welcome
Spread shade across the sultry way;
And not for him the fountain scatters
        Its smoke of spray.

And not for him shall misted grotto
Beckon as through a veil outspread,
Nor dewy dust from waters falling
        Refresh his head.

My God, send down Thy consolation,
To him who, on life's stony street,
Like a poor beggar, past the garden
        Drags weary feet.

ANNA AKHMATOVA (1889–1966)

THE END

Noiseless they moved about the house,
        No hope was in their eyes.
They brought me to the dying man
        I could not recognise.

'Thank God!' he said. Then more remote
        And sunk in thought he grew.
'I know it's time I went: but first
        I had to wait for you;

'For every word you ever said
        Through my delirium ran –
· Tell me: of course you can't forgive?'
        I looked, and said: 'I can.'

It seemed that suddenly the walls
          From floor to ceiling shone,
And lit the silken coverlet
          His dry hand lay upon.

The predatory head thrown back
          Was coarsened fearfully;
Through the dark bitten lips no sound
          Of breathing came to me.

Then, all at once, the last strength leapt
          In those blue eyes half-blind:
'It's good that you will let me go:
          You were not always kind.'

Again I recognised the face,
          Grown younger for release.
I said: 'Thy servant lettest Thou,
          O Lord, depart in peace.'

ALEXANDER ALEXANDROVICH BLOK (1880-1921)

IN THE CATHEDRAL CHOIR

In the cathedral choir a girl stood singing
Of all the weary on an alien shore,
Of all the ships gone to sea, and of all people
Who can remember happiness no more.

Her voice went soaring in the cupola,
And, listening in the darkness, everyone
Saw how the sunlight touched her on the shoulder,
And how her white dress sang in a shaft of sun.

It seemed to all that happiness was coming;
The ships had reached a haven free from harm;
And in the strange land all the tired people
Had found a life of brightness and of calm.

Sweet voice...thin beam...Only a child is crying
High up outside the sanctuary door,
Partaker of the mystery, understanding
That nobody will come back any more.

BORN IN THE YEARS OF SLOTH

Born in the years of sloth and dull decay,
Men quite forgot their way and all they met.
We, who are sons of Russia's dreadful day,
We never can forget.

Destroying days, of which the memory sears;
What did they bode? Our hope, or final ill?
For on our faces from those smouldering years
There is a red light still.

Now by the tocsin's ever-echoing din;
We are struck mute. Once ardent and up-buoyed,
Our hearts are faithless, and most deep within
There is a fatal void.

Come at the hour of death, you croaking horde
Swarm on us, ravens, lying sick and dumb!
Those who are worthier, O Lord, O Lord,
Shall see Thy kingdom come.